WOMEN ON THE BIBLICAL ROAD

Ruth, Naomi, and the Female Journey

Mishael Maswari Caspi
Rachel S. Havrelock

University Press of America, Inc.
Lanham • New York • London

Copyright © 1996 by
University Press of America,® Inc.
4720 Boston Way
Lanham, Maryland 20706

3 Henrietta Street
London, WC2E 8LU England

ISBN 0-7618-0279-7 (cloth: alk. ppr.)
ISBN 0-7618-0280-0 (pbk: alk. ppr.)

For Gila and Ika–With my love
(MMC).

To my road companions, phantasmal and real
(RSH).

Table of Contents

Acknowledgments

In 1991, Professor Henry Thompson challenged me to prepare an annotated bibliography for the book of Ruth. That project led to this one, so I thank him. Professor Murray Baumgarten provided us with guidance and argument which has improved our work. Gildas Hamel lent his excellent perception and valuable comments to the work. I thank Kenneth Kramer for the Sunday meetings where we read the text over and over again and for the creative questions he asked. I also acknowledge a very dear person, Hassane Bauhaja, for his insight and wise counsel. (MMC)

It has been my greatest journey to date: a climbing of mountains, crossing of rivers, and chasing of a God who makes her appearance in fire and dreams. I have gathered at the well, sung out in response to Miriam, and spent long days gathering wheat in the fields.

I embarked on the biblical road three years ago when Professor Mishael Caspi first told me to begin giving serious consideration to the book of Ruth. I expected a short jaunt through a story which had bothered me as a child. I had never been comfortable with what I perceived as Ruth's submission. Planning to write a criticism of biblical patriarchy, I approached the story and discovered things far different from my childhood perception.

Ruth the Moabite was denied to me as a girl. I was taught to heroize men like Abraham, Jacob, and David while humbling myself to a male God. I rediscovered Ruth and her road around the same time I realized that God is as much female as she is male. I offer Ruth as a hero, a remarkable traveler, a woman whose name to sound.

I thank Jacob Estes, Shira Sergant, and Rhoda Stamell for their assistance in editing, Rachel Kubby for the use of her computer, Jenny Raven for her encouragement, and Virgina Eubanks for her cyber-help. All for their inspiration. (RSH)

FOREWORD

The book you are about to read examines the story in the Hebrew Bible we call "The Book of Ruth." Professors Caspi and Havrelock have thought deeply about the Ruth and Naomi story, a story told and retold by generations of Hebrew women before it was written down by one author, herself a woman. Their literary analysis of this story is simultaneously fanciful, solid, and provocative. For scholars of the Hebrew Bible, there is a careful, analytic examination of various narratives in Genesis and how they set the stage for the narrative of Ruth and Naomi. Caspi and Havrelock show us how the male and female story cycles in Genesis are synthesized in the Ruth and Naomi story. The separate stands of Abraham, Sarah, Hagar, Isaac, Rebekah, and Rachel become intertwined in alternating narratives of masculine prowess and female barrenness, of female determination and ingenuity and masculine journeying without direction, of masculine conflict which requires separation and murder and of female conflict which must somehow be managed because the women, quite simply, cannot leave.

The basic human narrative of birth, separation, and death here is shown as the basis of all biblical stories, a narrative trinity of origin, separation, and return. These basic elements of the life cycle are the skeleton of every Biblical narrative that the authors read closely. These elements, like the masculine and feminine elements distinguished in the stories in Genesis, come together (in a way resembling the double helix of DNA) in the story of Ruth and Naomi.

If the masculine characters in Genesis embody separation in murder, fights, leaving the country for another land, and wandering, the feminine characters embody separation when they cannot bear children. When women are at "a loss" in Genesis, that is, when they are barren, we hear the most from them and see their lives most clearly, not obscured or hidden by the assertiveness (verbal and physical) of the masculine characters.

These stories of infertility give the authors a way to understand both the cyclical nature of Biblical narratives as well as a way to connect, both in lineage and in literary form, the stories in Genesis with the narrative in Ruth. The barrenness of matriarchs in Genesis first leads them to lament and to converse with one another, often in a call-and-response pattern; after their verbal expression of loss, they then act. These women are decisive and seek to change their infertility, in part because they wish to restore their relationships to God and to each other. We are left to ponder the difficult question of whether the authors of these narratives give us the laments of infertile women as a way of showing us women who are willing to protest loudly or whether the loss of these women sparks a different interest in the authors of the Biblical stories. Did the male authors wonder why these women turned to one another, even when the didn't like each other? Did these authors feel abandoned because they were not the central characters or did they hover on the edges of a female ceremony, trying to control it by describing it?

This book gives us the ability to ask these kinds of questions of the literature with perspicacious analysis of the specific elements, both aesthetic and structural, of the narratives. Jacob, Abraham and Isaac are clearly seekers who conduct their quests in an external landscape with uncertain relationships through wandering. The women, Sarah, Rebekah, Hagar, Miriam, understand their relationships to their bodies and to the earth in differing ways. The alienation of wandering the earth to try to find how to connect to God differs from the alienation of infertility. No matter how much these women might want to escape, they know that everywhere they go, they take themselves, their bodies, with them. Adam may be able to break with the soil following the expulsion from Eden, but Eve cannot break away from her body. Both men and woman in Israel journey to survive, to find food, water, and safety, but they journey differently. These journeys, symbolized and described differently in Genesis, gendered in Genesis, show up differently in Ruth.

The journey itself is physical and spiritual; the nourishment wandering may enable the seeker to connect with God. Since the Hebrew God is a transnational god, since the Hebrew God does not have a specific embodiment, since the Hebrew God is THE GOD and not a god among many fellow gods and goddesses, God may be in the terrain over which one wanders, or in the endometrium of the uterus. The authors claim that, at least originally, Hebrew monotheism wanted to show that all of life was not gendered. Yet, over time, as we know, the God of the Hebrew Bible seems to acquire mostly masculine characters and is profoundly misogynistic. Havrelock and Caspi remind us that the women of the Hebrew Bible would not have accepted such a masculinized notion of God and they outline a notion of God that is undifferentiated and is truly expansive. They show us that simple tricks with changing pronouns won't give us such a unified God.

While the men leave their families and friends and homes so that they can wander as isolated individuals to find and be with God in the Hebrew narratives, the woman make their journeys in pairs or in the company of other women. We have no Butch Cassidy and the Sundance Kid in these stories, but we do have many versions of Thelma and Louise. Interestingly, the women in the Hebrew Bible cannot create stirring narratives about their experiences that will go unchecked. Their descriptions of the world will be experienced and corroborated in the world of fellow speakers who are women. Sarah travels with Hagar, Rebekah travels with Devorah and Rachel and Leah travel together and stand by their man together.

The authors provide wonderfully literate analyses of the difference this companionship makes and also point to a politics that varies from what we see, for example, in the interactions of Cain and Able. They show us that despite the tensions in the stories of Sarah and Hagar and Rachel and Leah, the women stay together at least until they achieve their shared goal, the greater good, the establishment and continuity of the family. They remind us that the stories of the matriarchs that we have in Genesis are partial, fragmented, and reduced, and that we see these women blended into the narratives of the men in their lives. The stories of the women are subsumed in the heroic narratives of the male journeys and struggles (much as they are in Westerns). The examination of the symbolism of the mandrakes in Rachel and Leah's story here gives us a model of conflict facilitation rather different from the path chosen by Jacob and Esau. One of the results of this different path is that, although Rachel does not get to Bethlehem, her story makes it possible for Ruth to get there and complete the narrative cycle. Similarly, when Moses and Miriam celebrate the good fortune of their tribe, Moses narrates and Miriam engages. She and the women sing together and engage in call-and-response. Moses orates about the enemies of Israel and how they will be defeated.

The authors have persuaded me that the storyteller of Ruth knew about the ritual Miriam led. Ruth and Naomi, like the women at Miriam's assembly, move toward independence by departing from the male world. When Naomi, Orpah, and Ruth leave Moab, they leave sickness and move toward healing. They leave as a group and later dwindle to a couple after Orpah goes back to her mother's house but Ruth refuses to go. The analysis of the call-and-response of Ruth and Naomi you will read here is thrilling and the authors give us an analysis of power among equals that they wittily contrast with the "ten-step program" of Moses.

Leaving Moab enables Ruth and Naomi to discover their own voices and figure out what they think and how they feel. From this, new power comes. This new power is the progeny of their relationship. The Ruth the storyteller gives us is a woman who is feminine and masculine, nurturing and affectionate, strong and aggressive, smart and tough. She cannot be reduced to any of the usual gender stereotypes because she is a creature of harmony, balancing many roles and moving on down the road.

The Ruth we are able to see through Caspi's and Havrelock's eyes is a strong Moabite women who helps the Hebrews prosper and continue. If she is not the Victorian suffragette Elizabeth Cady Stanton provides in *The Woman's Bible* (how wonderful to see that oft-neglected text examined here), neither is she like the doomed heroines of "Thelma and Louise" (although I still wonder if the kiss that Louise planted on Thelma has any counterpart in the Ruth and Naomi relationship) who must die to become free from the evils of the patriarchal world which kept them and the world from freedom or God, depending on your preference.

In *Women on the Biblical Road: Ruth, Naomi, and the Female Journey*, Rachel Havrelock and Mishael Caspi locate and retrieve the lost ancient voices of female prophets. They see what Zora Neale Hurston saw when she wrote:

Ships at a distance have every man's wish on board. For some they come in with the tide. For others they sail forever on the horizon, never out of sight, never landing until the Watcher turns his eyes away in resignation, his dreams mocked to death by Time. That is the life of men.

Now women forget all those things they don't want to remember, and remember everything they don't want to forget. The dream is the truth. They they act and do things accordingly.

So the beginning of this was a woman and she had come back from burying the dead.

Their Eyes Were Watching God

Martha A. Crunkleton
Dean of the Faculty
Bates College

PREFACE

This book is intended as a guide through the stories of the Hebrew Bible. It maps the paths of female heroes and the terrains which they wander. Each chapter should be read in conjunction with the source text to which it refers: Chapter One-Genesis, Chapter Two-Exodus, Chapter Three-1 Kings. At the core of this look at women on the biblical road is the book of Ruth, the Bible's most complete tale of the female adventure. In many ways, the book of Ruth fills in the gaps of briefer and more fragmented women's stories. It is the focal point of Chapter Four as well as the book's locus. To map the story of Ruth, Chapter Four has been divided into terrains, or narrative landscapes through which Ruth and Naomi travel.

While the biblical world is far different from our own, there is something hauntingly familiar about the terrains of its journeys. While a contemporary hero may not be required to seek sustenance in wheat fields, she will inevitably have to face the source and meaning of her life. Biblical stories provide invaluable "road rules" for journeys of any time period. Whether wandering through the Sinai desert or traveling the information super-highway, the quest for companionship, new perception, and affiliation with larger powers endures. The journey, even when described by different cultures and time periods, is made of the same components. We have brought the women of the Bible into our time, in the hope that their journeys may help to elucidate our own.

CHAPTER ONE

THE BIBLICAL CYCLE

Of earth at large, whispering through medium of me;
(But I see the road continued, and the journey ever continued;)
                              –Walt Whitman

THE BIBLICAL CYCLE

The basis of biblical stories is a cycle of origination, separation, and return. Modeled after the life cycle, the same fundamental story is told again and again. Landscapes change, characters vary from "the first man and woman" to an entire nation, time passes, but the cycle endures. Recurring themes take their form in journey stories which chronicle the wanderings of biblical heroes.

There are two parallel traditions of journey stories: one in which biblical women realize the cycle as an inherent part of them and another in which the "founding fathers" go out on quests to discover the cycle in the world around them. Biblical women also embark on journeys away from their homes, but it is the movement from fertility to infertility which receives the most detailed description.

In the book of Ruth, the male and female cycles established in Genesis are synthesized. Ruth is a hero like Abraham and the founder of a nation like Sarah. The Book of Ruth strikes a balance between two parallel traditions as Ruth and Naomi walk the path between exile and home, famine and harvest, death and life. To understand the journey of Ruth and Naomi, we will first analyze the cycle of humanity in Genesis.

THE FEMALE JOURNEY

When biblical women are barren, the focus of the narrative shifts from the male journey to the female one. While giving birth does not comprise the entire female experience, it is during the crisis of infertility or after the joy of a birth that readers gain the most comprehensive account of the female value system. Beginning with Eve, biblical women inherit the impulse to create, or to act "in God's image" as givers of life. The movement from barrenness to pregnancy follows a cyclic pattern of departure and return. When biblical women are unable to give birth, it is attributed to the absence of God. In response to this absence, Sarah, Rebekah, and Rachel raise their voices in protest, have a direct encounter with God, and gain the ability to give birth.

In the Genesis cycles, women's bodies are the vehicle of communication with God. When the matriarchs conceive or are reminded of their ability to conceive (through menstruation), it is read as a sign of the alliance and support of God. Barrenness signifies God's absence or opposition and is a time when the desire to create is frustrated. This blockage is attributed to God withholding the power of creation. When Sarah is barren, she tells Abraham, "you see that the Lord has not allowed me to bear a child" (Gen. 16:2). The narrator of Rachel's story attributes her infertility to ongoing tension with God, "when the Lord saw that Leah was not loved, he granted her a child; but Rachel was childless" (Gen. 29:31). The physical condition of infertility becomes psychological as the women strive to understand the rift in their relationship to God and to alter the situation.

Barrenness sets the journey in motion. The journey's first step is a two-fold process of articulation and action. First, the matriarchs articulate their discontent in a statement of protest and then they take action. The matriarchs have been portrayed by writers of midrash and scholarship alike as the passive spectators of their husband's journeys. In his ironically titled book, *Assertive Biblical Women*, William E. Phipps claims that "Sarah passively endures much indignity from her husband."[1] Yet in the biblical text, Sarah plays an active role in defining her own destiny.

Sarah is a woman who wants immediate results. She not only

describes her discontent to Abraham, but also commands him to sleep with her maidservant Hagar. "'Take my slave-girl; perhaps I shall found a family (be built up) through her.' Abram agreed to what his wife said; so Sarai, Abram's wife, brought her slave-girl, Hagar the Egyptian, and gave her to her husband Abram as a wife" (Gen. 16: 2-3). The verb ibane (built up) indicates that Sarah is most interested in the continuity of her own lineage. She does not place faith in God's repeated promises to Abraham that his descendants will be like "stars in the sky." Sarah wants a practical solution to her infertility. Perhaps she also wants to test Abraham's virility. When Abraham impregnates Hagar, Sarah realizes that she is the one who is infertile. According to patriarchal standards, a barren woman has no value. Hagar uses this manner of thinking by "despising her mistress" once she becomes pregnant. To retaliate and reveal her power, Sarah "ill-treats" the Egyptian woman. The issue of motherhood drives the two women apart. A similar situation occurs in the story of Rachel and Leah and in the story of Solomon's judgment over two women. Only in the book of Ruth is shared motherhood lauded and celebrated as a manifestation of love.

Rebekah controls family business more furtively, directing the actions of her husband and sons. She sends Isaac to confront God and make her supplication by proxy. While the direct statement of protest to Isaac is not recorded, we can infer that one was made from his actions. "Isaac appealed to the Lord on behalf of his wife because she was barren, the Lord yielded to his entreaty, and Rebecca conceived" (Gen. 25:21). Perhaps Rebekah does not feel comfortable confronting her husband's God, referred to as "the Fear," and therefore delegates the responsibility. Still, Rebekah's perception that God has abandoned her becomes apparent in the language of Isaac's supplication.

In conjunction with Rachel's entire journey cycle, her mortification over being barren is inextricable from a competition with her sister. "When Rachel found that she bore Jacob no children, she became jealous of her sister and said to Jacob, 'give me sons, or I shall die.' Jacob said angrily to Rachel, 'Can I take the place of God who has denied you children?" (Gen. 30:1-2). Rachel makes her first statement of protest to Jacob, only to be told that the power to impregnate does not rest in his hands. Ilana Pardes views Rachel's demand as a plea for her own life, "in but a few words she conveys the unbearable agony of being a barren woman: childlessness means death".[2] Rachel cannot stand the thought of being devalued by her sister's success. Without children, Rachel feels like a ghost, as much dead as she is live. The urgency of her plea shows Rachel's fierce desire to be heard and to be counted in the family.

When her protest serves only to make Jacob angry, Rachel uses Sarah's approach and brings her maidservant to Jacob. "She said, 'Here is my slave-girl Bilhah. Lie with her, so that she may bear sons to be laid upon my knees, and through her I too may build up a family.' So she gave him her slave-girl Bilhah as a wife, and Jacob lay with her" (Gen. 30: 3-4). Rachel's language and actions mirror Sarah's as they both attempt to build a legacy through the children of their maidservants. The statement of protest and the insistence that their servants become surrogate mothers signal to God that Sarah, Rebekah, and Rachel want to have children by any means necessary. God responds by visiting with the women and acceding to their desire. These meetings are divine encounters in which the matriarchs have the opportunity to challenge, barter, and negotiate with God in exchange for the ability to give birth.

Sarah confronts the divine during the "three-in-one" visitation of angels to her tent. By the time the angels appear, Sarah is post-menopausal and has probably accepted her infertility. The mysterious guests speak to Abraham and assure him, "About this time next year, I will be sure to come back to you and Sarah your wife shall have a son" (Gen. 18:10). Sarah stands by the door of her tent and eavesdrops. She does not question the fact that strangers are discussing her body, but distrusts what they promise. She laughs and mumbles to herself, "I am past bearing children now that I am out of my time, and my husband is old" (Gen. 18:12).

God, in turn, overhears and reveals Sarah's laughter to Abraham by asking him, "'Why did Sarah laugh and say, Shall I indeed bear a child when I am old? Is anything impossible for the Lord? In due season I will come back to you, about this time next year, and Sarah shall have a son." Sarah denies her laughter, but God responds, "Yes you did laugh" (Gen. 18:13-15). In this scene, Sarah and God play listening games. Sarah listens in disbelief to God's promise and God listens in on Sarah's interior dialogue. With these games, Sarah and God are entering into each others trust.

During Rebekah's pregnancy, she is plagued with "the children press(ing) hard on each other in her womb." She interprets this sensation as symbolic and goes to consult an oracle. "So she went to seek guidance of the Lord. If this is how it is with me, What does it mean?" Her query is answered with a riddle: "Two nations in your womb, two peoples, going their own ways from birth! one shall be stronger than the other; the older shall be servant to the younger" (Gen. 25: 22-23). Rebekah receives a prophecy regarding the children forming inside of her. By providing her with this information, God conspires to ensure that the prophecy comes true. From birth, Rebekah favors Jacob and takes all the necessary steps to make him "stronger than the other."

After Rachel has tried supplication, substitution, and aphrodisiacs (mandrakes), God intervenes and fulfills her quest. "Then God thought of Rachel; he heard her prayer and gave her a child; so she conceived and bore a son" (Gen. 30:22). God's conception of Rachel allows her to conceive. Wrestling with barrenness is the means by which God tests the matriarchs. This trial, passed from generation to generation, may well be the legacy of a priestess.

The repeated motif of barrenness signals that the struggle between body and mind is of primary importance in the female journey. In *Sarah the Priestess*, Savina Teubal suggests that Sarah's initial inability to have children indicates her role as a priestess. Priestesses in the ancient near-eastern world were not expected to bear children until after they had a direct encounter with the god or goddesses they served.

> All three matriarchs bore their children late in life, Sarah and Rebekah having one pregnancy and Rachel two. It is interesting that the stories of Sarah and Rebekah were left almost intact, with only a slight change of focus, so that their barrenness necessitated divine intervention to conform to the patriarchal adage given to Noah; "Be fertile and increase and fill the earth."[3]

Whether or not Sarah, Rebekah, and Rachel are priestesses, they must develop their own relationship with God before giving birth. The time without children may be a period of observation in which God tests the women to determine if they are able to be his partners in the creation of life. God aside, not having children provides Sarah, Rebekah, and Rachel with a period of personal exploration and evolution. As readers, we become acquainted only with the trauma of barrenness. This may be because barrenness becomes significant when the women protest the situation or because this stage of the female journey is of interest to male narrators.

After giving birth, the power of female creation is celebrated in a naming ceremony. In this uniquely female assembly, the women of the community surround the new mother and give her the opportunity to describe the journey of her conception. The name of the child indicates a pivotal point of the mother's experience and determines the character of the child. Savina Teubal suggests that an oral tradition handed down from generation to generation is made implicit in narrative genealogies. "I suspect that all the births in Genesis originally have a naming story attached."[4] In the naming scenes, we can see traces of longer stories.

After Isaac's birth, Sarah admits to laughing when she overheard the promise of a child. "The Lord showed favor to Sarah as he had promised, and made good what he had said about her ... Sarah said, 'God has given me good reason to laugh, and everybody who hears will laugh with me'" (Gen. 21: 2,6). On a personal level, this is Sarah's statement of overriding joy, but to the community, this is Sarah's statement of renewed faith. She attributes her laughter to a miracle performed by God and declares, "'Whoever would have told Abraham that Sarah would suckle children? Yet I have borne him a son for his old age'" (Gen. 21:6-7). If Sarah is, in fact, a priestess, then this may be a speech given to women on the fulfillment of impossible wishes.

Midwives played an integral role in the birth process by providing medical as well as psychological guidance. The involvement of midwives becomes apparent in the collective voice which names the children. When Rebekah's twins are born, the midwives assisting her join in the naming ceremony. "When her time had come, there were indeed twins in her womb. The first came out Red, hairy all over like a hair-cloak, and they named him Esau. Immediately afterwards his brother was born with his hand grasping Esau's heel, and they called him Jacob" (Gen. 25: 24-26). The names of the twins indicate the prophecy received by Rebekah. The "they" in this passage is the assembly of women surrounding Rebekah after she gives birth.

Rachel and Leah express their competition in their children's naming ceremonies. In an exclusively female environment, they can engage in a dialogue which resolves their tension enough to not interfere with the larger family structure. When her maidservant conceives, Rachel has an opportunity to respond to the repeated jibes contained in the names of Leah's children.

Rachel said, "God has given judgment for me; he has indeed heard me and given me a son," so she named him Dan. Rachel's slave-girl Bilhah again conceived and bore Jacob another son. Rachel said, "I have played a fine trick on my sister, and it has succeeded"; so she named him Naphtali. When Leah found that she was bearing no more children, she took her slave-girl Zilpah and gave her to Jacob as a wife, and Zilpah bore Jacob a son. Leah said, "Good fortune has come," and she named him Gad. Zilpah, Leah's slave-girl, bore Jacob another son, and Leah said, "Happiness has come, for young women will call me happy." So she named him Asher (Gen. 30:5-13).

The irony of this scene is that Rachel and Leah busy themselves with naming children that belong to them only by proxy.

After Rachel is remembered by God and gives birth to Joseph, she immediately asks God for a second child. In Joseph's naming ceremony, she says, "'God has taken away my humiliation.' She named him Joseph saying, 'May the Lord add another son!'" (Gen. 30:24). The name of each of Jacob's twelve sons bears some element of the sisters' rivalry. This carries over into the enormous jealousy that Leah's ten sons bear toward Joseph.

The power of midwives in Hebraic tradition is reinforced in the story of Rachel's death. During tremendous labor pains, Rachel's midwife eases her suffering with words of comfort. "While her pains were upon her, the midwife said, 'Do not be afraid, this is another son for you.' Then with her last breath, as she was dying, she named him Ben-oni" (Gen. 35:17-18). In this scene, it is not the child that the midwife is concerned with, but Rachel. This intimacy between the two women is apparent in their last words.

In the story of Tamar, another "twin" birth, the voice of naming is attributed to the midwife.

When her time was come, there were twins in her womb, and while she was in labour one of them put out a hand the midwife took a scarlet thread and fastened it round the wrist, saying, "This one appeared first." No sooner had he drawn back his hand, then his brother came out and the midwife said, "What!" you have broken out first!' So he was named Perez. Soon afterwards his brother was born with the scarlet thread on his wrist, and he was named Zerah. (Gen. 38:27-30)

The midwives' account of the birth determines the children's' names. Tamar's subversion of the patriarchal order is marked in the ambiguous order of her sons' birth. Perhaps the story which the midwives tell is a parable of Tamar's own experience.

The importance of midwifes culminates in the story of Shiprah and Puah. Pharaoh orders Shiprah and Puah, two Israelite midwives to kill all male babies. Shiprah and Puah display power comparable to Pharaoh's when they are called before him to answer for their disobedience. "They told Pharaoh that Hebrew women were not like Egyptian women. When they were in labor they gave birth before the midwife could get to them" (Ex. 1:19).

By opposing Pharaoh's decree, Shiprah and Puah preserve the sanctity of female assembly and the Israelite lineage.

In the book of Ruth, the midwife duties are performed by the "female chorus," a group of women who surround Naomi. The chorus first appears to welcome Naomi back to Bethlehem and again to name Ruth's child, but remain primarily concerned with Naomi's transformation. In the initial scene, Naomi feels defeated and cries out against God; in the final one, she holds a child against her bosom. Through the intimate dialogue of these scenes, the storyteller shows the importance of the support offered by a female community. Female gatherings frame the tale of Naomi in Bethlehem.

The female journey cycle takes its form, or its "geometry" from the menstrual cycle. The larger journey is modeled after the monthly cycle which allows women to create life. When Rachel's father enters her tent in search of his stolen household gods, she tells him not to approach her because she is on *derekh nashim*–"the journey of women," literally "having her period" (Gen. 31:35). Sarah speaks of her period as *orah nashim*–"the way of women." The word *orah* shares the same root with the word *oreah,* meaning guest. There is the sense in Sarah's description that she views her period as a divine guest similar to the ones who appear at her tent bearing promises.

Female alliance with God is directly tied to the menstrual cycle. Each month, when they bleed, women are reminded of their ability to create. The more that they understand about their individual cycle, the more they understand about the power to create gained by Eve's rebellion. While the desire for children leads the matriarchs into negotiations with God, giving birth solidifies this alliance. The relationship with God is not for themselves alone. Biblical women form partnerships with God to pass on to their children–to keep the cycle going.

THE MALE JOURNEY

The male heroes of the Bible are seekers. Since the cycle is not as apparent in their body's changes as it is in their wives', they must look outside of them for its manifestation. Abraham, Isaac, and Jacob move from place to place probing their external environment for signs of God. Through their wanderings, they discover the cycle of the day, of the seasons, and of experience. By learning these cycles, the men of the Bible come to understand the cyclic nature of the divine.

The quest is never completed because a state of return always leads to another departure. Throughout their journeys, God assures Abraham, Isaac, and Jacob that the land which they traverse will one day belong to their descendants. Acquisition of the land becomes part of securing God's promise. The drive to continue moving, continue searching, and continue settling is passed down through generations. Biblical stories describe the ongoing search of a people.

Before examining any other biblical journey story, one must first look to Genesis to gain an understanding of the journey sequence. On a microcosmic level, each character in Genesis follows his or her own cycle of leaving home, hitting the road, and developing a relationship to God. The narrative cycle of Genesis follows humanity's origin in the Garden of Eden and the estrangement from God caused by Adam, Cain, and Noah. After the construction of the Tower of Babel, the separation between humanity and God culminates in humanity being "scattered abroad upon the face of all the earth" (Gen. 11:9).

Genesis then describes the return to God through the wanderings of Abraham, Isaac, and Jacob. This cycle of return is completed when God renames Jacob as Israel. In the renaming, Jacob's identity is fused with the land he inhabits and his mission as founder of a nation. Adam makes the first break from the soil and Jacob returns to a state of co-habitation with the earth. This relationship is reflected in Jacob's sharing of a name with the place where he lives. Jacob's return, however, does not result in stability but leads to Joseph's departure to Egypt and the consequent resettlement of the whole family.

OUT OF EDEN

God's first action in Genesis is to create the world. His second is its destruction. Being made in "the image of God," Man and Woman share the same impulses. Adam is created from the dust of the earth (in Hebrew *adamah* means soil). Eve (mother of all living things) is life. The archetypes of Woman and Man come into being within a protected environment, a divine womb in which the four rivers represent the amniotic fluid. In this womb, Adam and Eve are nourished through no labor of their own.

In The Garden of Eden, there is nothing missing and nothing extra.

It is an undisturbed ecosystem whose wholeness makes it paradise. Adam and Eve are an integral part of this system in which a tree is as important as a man. In The Garden, there is no separation between environment and consciousness. Not only do Adam and Eve live in Eden, they think in Edenic terms. The language of their minds is a language of paradise. Their lack of inner disturbance prevents them from disturbing their lifeplace. "No plant of the field was yet in the earth, and no herb of the field had yet grown" (Gen. 2:5). Adam and Eve make no attempts at production. What grows, grows naturally as Eve and Adam only do what comes naturally. They are sustained without creating.

The womb-like nature of Eden frustrates Eve's desire to create. Paradise confines her. God has neither appeared to Eve, nor acknowledged her curiosities. When the snake appears, he offers a counter-challenge, "on the day you eat of it, then your eyes shall be opened and you shall be as gods, knowing good and evil" (Gen. 2: 4-5). Because it provides a means of escape, the snake's recommendation is acknowledged. Eve's eating of the fruit is a rebellion against Eden's limitations: the stage of protest within her journey . Eve tests the boundaries of the system and places personal knowledge above the code–an action which causes her expulsion from paradise.

The snake's option is presented in turn to Adam. A dialogue of disobedience begins which permanently alters the Edenic relationship. Eating of the fruit marks the end of a protected state. Adam and Eve leave the womb and are reborn as autonomous beings with the power to create and destroy. Adam becomes more detached from the soil and begins his own maturation process. God says to him: "Because thou hast hearkened to the voice of thy wife and hast eaten of the tree, of which I commanded thee saying thou shalt not eat of it: cursed is the ground for thy sake" (Gen. 2:17). Because Adam chose to develop his breath of life, his body is cursed (ground = Adam(ah)).

The curse is that Adam's physical existence becomes one of toil. Three conditions define the new relationship: "in sorrow shalt thou eat of it all the days of thy life," "thorns also and thistles shall it bring forth to thee: and thou shalt eat of the herb of the field," and "in the sweat of thy face shalt thou eat bread" (Gen. 2:18). Outside of Eden, Adam must labor to survive. With labor, Adam learns struggle and pain. It soon becomes clear to Adam that only through similar trials will he reap the harvest of the divine.

Adam's labor symbolizes humanity's first separation from God who is understood in terms of the earth's conditions. In Eden, God was manifest as the creator/provider who nurtured Adam and Eve. When they separate from the Edenic "womb," struggle is incorporated as part of their relationship to the land. In the midst of struggle, God seems absent. Adam measures his distance from God by the amount of pain he encounters in his labor. "You shall gain your bread by the sweat of your brow until you return to the ground" (Gen. 3:19).

Eve's first action outside of the garden is to create. The birth of her first son is preceded by an encounter with God and followed by a naming ceremony. "And the man knew Eve his wife and she conceived and gave birth to Cain and said, 'I bought a man of God'" (Gen. 4:1) (ot). We imagine this transaction taking place in a type of divine marketplace where Eve barters with God for the ability to create. Eve and God have a relationship of mutual testing. We imagine them haggling and debating over the price of a child until they make a deal that Eve can give birth if she can withstand the pain of labor. God says to her, "I will increase your labor and your groaning, and in labor you shall bear children" (Gen. 3:16). Where Adam communicates with God through the soil, Eve understands divine power through her body's changes. Pain in childbirth is the struggle which runs parallel to Adam's labor in the soil.

Outside of Eden, Eve not only has the power to create, but she also has a voice to describe this power. Her statement can be translated as "I bought a man of God," or "I have created a man equally with God" (Gen. 4:1). Eve gives testimony to her acquisition of divine power by speaking in terms of her encounter with God. The fact that she creates life and expresses this creation in terms of an interaction with God proves that, for her, the post-Edenic separation is almost non-existent. Leaving Eden may in fact have been her greatest liberation. Outside of the Garden, Eve can realize her independence in her own ability to create. When one of her sons murders the other, she responds by giving birth to a third child. Cain's destruction is checked by Eve's creation. In this naming ceremony, Eve says "I will call him Seth because God has planted in me another seed in place of Abel who was killed by Cain" (Gen. 4:25).

THE MARK OF CAIN

Cain's murder causes the second separation from God. Cain is "a tiller of the soil" who spends his days in direct contact with the earth (Gen. 4:3). Cain labors in the soil as prescribed in his father's punishment. And like his father, Cain reads the character of God through the features of the earth. Cain's relationship to God is direct and dynamic.

Cain initiates the ritual of offering, "the day came when Cain brought some of the produce of the soil as a gift to the Lord" (Gen. 4:4). His brother Abel, "a shepherd" who spends his days wandering with his flocks. "also" brings an offering. God accepts Abel's offering and rejects Cain's. In response, Cain looks "downward" to the earth and is instructed by God: "If you do well, you are accepted; if not, sin is a demon crouching at the door. It shall be eager for you, and you will be mastered by it" (Gen. 4:7). Rather than soothing him, God's voice emanating from the ground inflames his anger.

Cain responds by leading his brother to "the field" and murdering him. When God confronts Cain about his actions, he denies them, but God calls the earth as his witness. "Your brother's blood that has been shed is crying out to me from the ground" (Gen. 4:10). Because Cain has tainted the soil with blood, blood stands between him and God. God says, "Now you are accursed, and banished from the ground which has opened its (her) mouth wide to receive your brother's blood, which you have shed" (Gen. 4:11). The feminine personification of the ground raises several questions. The ground is used as the medium of communication between God and Cain, but here God refers to a separate divinity opening her mouth to drink Abel's blood. Was the soil understood as a female goddess able to accept seed as well as blood? Is this female "ground-figure" part of God or a separate entity? Does this ground-figure mediate relationships between humanity and God?

Cain does not find out because he is banished from the earth. He is denied his livelihood as well as his connection to God. God says, "when you till the ground, it will no longer yield you its (her) wealth" (Gen. 4:12). He is condemned to a state of conflict with the world. "You shall be a vagrant and a wanderer on earth" (Gen. 4:12). Cain's wandering becomes a constant reminder of his transgression. His impulse toward creation cannot be expressed by "tilling the earth," or by growing food.

Cain tries to conceal his cursed relationship by building a city. "Cain was then building a city, which he named Enoch after his son" (Gen. 4:17). Cain's creative impulse is displaced from growing food to building structures. He hopes that the construction of a city will protect him from his curse. "Cain means 'ownership.' Ownership was the originator of the earthly city."[5] As Adam passed his curse to Cain, Cain transmits the legacy of exile to Enoch.

The midrash of Genesis Rabbah describes this gradual separation in terms of the Shekhina's departure.

R. Abba b. Kahana said: Not Mehallek but Mith-halek is written here, which means that it leaped and ascended. The real home of the Shekhina was in the nether sphere; when Adam sinned it departed to the first rakia, (firmament); when Cain sinned, it ascended to the second rakia; when the generation of Enoch sinned, it ascended to the third: when the generation of the flood sinned, to the fourth; with the generation of the separation to the sixth, with the Egyptians in the days of Abraham, to the seventh. But as against these there arose seven righteous men: Abraham, Isaac, Jacob, Levi, Kehath, Amram, and Moses, and they brought it down again to the earth. Abraham from the seventh to the sixth, Isaac from the sixth to the fifth, Jacob from the fifth to the fourth, Levi from the fourth to the third, Kohath from the third to the second, Amram from the second to the first, while Moses brought it right down below.[6]

In Talmudic literature, the Shekhina represents the aspect of the divine which appears on earth. According to Raphael Patai, "the Shekhina concept stood for an independent, feminine divine entity prompted by her compassionate nature to argue with God in defense of man."[7] The Shekhina represents the divinity of the earth itself. She is the womb which receives seed and creates life. In the above story, the Shekina's ascent from the earth runs parallel to humanity's increasing distance from a relationship of intimacy with the land.

The descendants of Cain populate the earth. When God looks at his creation, he sees that mankind's "thoughts and inclinations were always evil. He was sorry that he had made man on earth, He was grieved at heart" (Gen. 6:6). Humanity's destructive impulse takes form in violence and corruption. God reacts with His own show of violence. "This race of man whom I have created, I will wipe them off the face of the earth–man and beast, I am sorry that I ever made them" (Gen. 6:7). God uses water to destroy humanity and to cleanse the earth of corruption. Since the "earth is teeming with violence," God wants a comprehensive cleansing of all his creations.

The only person on earth who "finds favor in God's eyes" is Noah, meaning "comfort" in Hebrew (Gen. 6:8) (ot). In the flood story which chronicles a comprehensive destruction, there is little mention of women. Of Noah's wife, we know only that she comes with him into the ark. Female creation does not appear in this story of destruction. Noah is even given full responsibility for the birth of his sons. "And Noah gave birth to three sons: Shem, Ham, and Yefet" (Gen. 6:10). Noah is the person chosen to create his own life-saving vessel and to survive the flood.

> Said the Holy One, blessed be He: If these which have neither mouth nor speech, no thus, how just more will I be praised when I create man! But the generation of Enoch arose and rebelled against Him. The generation of the Flood and that of the Separation arose and rebelled against Him. Thereupon the Holy One blessed be He said: Let these be removed and the former come. Hence it is written, "And the Lord said I will blot out man." What do they think? That I need armies? Did I not create the world with a word? I will utter a word and destroy them. R. Berakhiah said, surely I created them from the earth. What dissolves earth? Water. Then let the water come and dissolve the earth. R. Levi said in R. Johanan's name: Even the nether stone of a millstone was dissolved.[8]

To cleanse the soil of the blood spilled by Cain's murder and the corruption festering in the cities, God uses water–the best solvent. Noah is instructed to erase the wicked past from his thoughts in the same manner that God washes the corrupt population from the earth. Noah's mission is to use the time of the flood as a period of self-reflection and then to emerge from the ark and found a renewed nation. God says to him, "I intend to bring the waters of the flood over the earth to destroy every human being under heaven that has the spirit of life; everything on earth shall perish. But with you I will make a covenant, and you shall go into the ark, you and your sons, your wife and your sons' wives with you" (Gen. 6: 17-18). God attributes the wickedness of humanity to the "breath of life" with which He endowed them and hopes to negate corruption on the earth by destroying the population who inherited this original breath. During the period of complete cleansing, Noah and his family are protected in the womb-like structure of the ark. In sealing Noah and his family from the effects of the flood, God seeks a microcosmic recreation of Eden. The balance is represented by Noah's bringing "two of every kind" into the ark (Gen. 6:19).

The waters of the flood are both deadly and restorative. Noah does not directly experience these elements because he is contained within the ark. "And the Lord closed the door on him" (Gen. 7:16). Again, God does not allow Noah to develop a dialogic relationship with Him. Noah is instructed to wait in incubation until he can emerge and conduct God's agenda on restored soil.

After the waters have subsided, God promises Noah that He will never destroy the earth again. Instead, a cyclical process will maintain a balance. "While the earth lasts, seed time and harvest, and cold and heat, summer and winter, day and night shall never cease" (Gen. 8:22). With this promise, God's intervention into human life is minimized and blended into the balance of nature.

Noah's "fall" occurs when he emerges from the ark into the cleansed world and plants a vineyard. According to Jewish legend, Noah's transgression is that he planted a vineyard to give himself pleasure rather than a tree whose fruits would be enjoyed by his descendants. This planting represents a desire to escape from duty. Not mindful of the divine mission, Noah plants for his own comfort. This action is similar to Eve's decision to eat of the fruit. As Eve strove to be God-like, Noah seeks his personal fulfillment. The midrash proposes an alliance in Noah's case similar to Adam's and Eve's acceptance of the serpent's suggestion: "As he was going to plant the vineyard the demon Shimadon met him and proposed:

'Come into partnership with me in this vineyard, but take care not to enter into my portion, for if you do I will injure you.'"[9] In this midrashic story as in the Eden story, an adversary is integral in the persuasion of deviance. In both cases, an alternate allegiance weakens the commitment to God. The midrash of Noah and the demon may seek to describe the struggle within Noah between what God tells him is right and what gives him pleasure. No matter how tightly God seals the ark, Noah is a product of his environment and age. Born in a violent and decadent time, Noah cannot remain completely untouched by these influences. Apparently he transcends violence, but decadence remains ingrained in his being. He makes an alliance with a demon, gets drunk, and incurs the wrath of God.

The agent of God's wrath is Noah's youngest son who "goes backward" and "humiliates his father." This act of incestuous sodomy may be seen as Noah's punishment for his drunkenness. According to Midrash: "... and he drank of the vine, and was drunken. He drank, immediately became intoxicated, and was thus put to shame. R. Hiyya b. Abba said: He planted it, drank thereof, and was humiliated all on one and the same day.[10] Noah's action results in the third separation from God. Because Noah did not use foresight in his choice of crops, his descendants inherit shortsightedness. God has vowed to never again destroy the earth, so He must learn to tolerate wickedness.

The descendants of Noah use their creative power to construct the Tower of Babel. They hope to reach the metaphoric height of God by producing a tall building. "'Come, they said, 'let us build ourselves a city and a tower with its top in the heavens, and make a name for ourselves'" (Gen. 11:3). This generation believes that their buildings are representative of their power, when in actuality the buildings show a lack of vision and a limited concept of "reaching heaven."

The construction of Babel causes an even greater separation. "So the Lord scattered them abroad from there upon the face of all the earth: and they ceased to build the city" (Gen. 11:8). The result of this scattering is the development of different languages which leads to misunderstanding between different peoples. Thus the separation exists on three different plains: between humanity and God, between humanity and the land, and between different cultural groups.

WOMEN AND MEN OF THE ROAD

Out of humanity's separation from God comes a process of return which spans three generations: Abraham and Sarah, Rebekah and Isaac, and Jacob, Rachel and Leah. The story of each generation is a cycle of its own, and together these stories describe the re-establishment of a working relationship with God.

Abraham, Isaac, and Jacob are men of the road. Like Huck Finn or Kerouac's Sal Paradise, they are dedicated to a life of wandering and an ethic of the road. The road, or the "way" (*Haderekh*) walked by Abraham, Isaac, and Jacob is the means of redeeming the estranged relationship to the land caused by Adam, Cain, and Noah. Their connection to the ground which they traverse is a promise by God that the land is intended for their descendants. The features of the land (mountains, groves, bodies of water) become symbolic of a journey toward greater intimacy with God. Parallel to the physical wanderings, each patriarch has a series of visions which inform their journeys.

Ancient people wandered to survive. They followed seasonal harvests and went where they were sure to find food. Such wanderings, as described in Genesis, are not only about food, but also about the construction of identity. Because Abraham, Isaac, and Jacob do not inhabit a specific town or area, they cannot define themselves in strictly geographic terms. They must forge a "road" identity strong enough to sustain them in unknown territory. The formation of this identity has implications beyond the personal. As the voice of God reminds them, they are paving the way for a nation. Their identity must be flexible enough to allow them to settle alongside other peoples and resilient enough to be passed down to future generations.

The patriarchs have no preconceived sense of boundary. Their wanderings span diverse ecological and cultural regions. Any sense of border is a direct result of the journey itself. When Abraham, Isaac, and Jacob stop at a sacred grove of trees, on a mountain, or alongside a stream, they sense the presence of God. When they flee to established urban centers during times of famine, they encounter disaster, usually in the form of a foreign king taking their wives. The patriarchs come to associate hardship with exile and pass this association to their descendants.

The patriarchs must split from the comforts of stability and live on the peripheries of communities in order to preserve a separate identity. As Adam had to leave Eden in order to gain the ability to create and to destroy, the patriarchs must sacrifice the stability of home to create a new tradition. God looks to the patriarchs to fulfill his agenda and they seek a similar sense of continuity in their sons. Since the legacy of the journey is passed down to the next generation, no individual ever sees its completion.

A WEIGHTLESS GOD:
MONOTHEISM AS NOMADIC SPIRITUALITY

The nomadic lifestyle of the patriarchs made it impossible for them to place their belief in regional deities. Since Abraham, Isaac, and Jacob were not bound to a specific region, their faith could not be directed toward place-specific gods. According to Savina Teubal, "ancient divinities were usually associated with specific regions ... this means that each region had its own distinctive beliefs."[11] In contrast, the Hebrew God had no specific physical manifestation. God was apparent only as a voice, a sense of presence, or in terms of angelic messengers. The forefathers realized these manifestations as aspects of a force assigned the name 'God.' In the absence of image, their God became a flexible concept able to be carried from hilltops, through valleys, and across streams.

Nomadic people cannot uphold a tradition of honoring household gods because they have no established household. *Teraphim,* or household gods made of stone or wood, would be cumbersome to people on the move. Instead of carrying gods with them, the patriarchs marked a resting point on their journey by building altars to God out of the materials at hand. "Abram passed through the country to the sanctuary at Shechem, the terebinth-tree of Moreh ... There the Lord appeared to Abram and said, 'I give this land to your descendants.' So Abram built an altar there to the Lord who appeared to him." (Gen. 12:6-8)

Savina Teubal explains that "travelers paid respect to local divinities whose regional protection they sought. Abraham did so at the sacred Canaanite terebinth tree of Moreh ("teacher" or "diviner") when he was in the vicinity of Shechem."[12] While Abraham entered this Canaanite holy place in search of the sacred, it is doubtful that he sought the protection or advice of the Canaanite deity. Rather, he used a Canaanite holy place to call upon his own God. Wherever Abraham traveled, God was accessible.

According to Patai, God "can easily cross international frontiers and establish himself in a new country."[13] The Hebraic concept of God is specifically designed for such transference. He is the God of wanderers, The God of the way. Lacking a specific embodiment, the divine is understood in terms of the terrain. While being part of the landscape, God becomes an inherent part of the journey.

Monotheism provided an expanded view of the sacred. In place of sun gods, water gods, war gods, and conception gods, there is one God who can be characterized by sun, water, war, and birth. This is not to say that polytheistic religions did not crossover and influence monotheistic beliefs. On the contrary, polytheism is consistently intertwined with the development of Hebrew monotheism (Rachel stealing her father's *teraphim,* the golden calf at the base of Mt. Sinai). Polytheism had a tremendous effect on Hebrew culture especially in the more settled times of the judges and the monarchy. "The very manner in which Solomon's temple was built in Jerusalem was conducive to the establishment of a polytheistic-syncretistic cult."[14]

The struggle and subsequent blending of poly and monotheistic belief systems is one of the primary tensions in the Hebrew Bible. The first commandment states, "You shall have no other gods before me," not "you shall have no other gods." Mythology, whether it speaks of one God or many, performs the same function: to forge bonds between people and the place they inhabit. Northrop Frye cites two "principles which myth uses in assimilating nature to human form: analogy and identity– analogy establishes parallels between human life and natural phenomena –identity conceives of a 'sun god' or 'a tree god.'"[15] The philosophy of Hebrew monotheism employs the technique of analogy to tell the combined story of a people and a land. The connection between human life and nature is reinforced by the notion that God has forged this bond. Divinity is read by the text of the land.

What Hebrew monotheism originally sought to portray was that all aspects of life are interrelated. Each experience or vision leads to a larger understanding and each fragment of life is unified in a larger whole. In theory, the idea that all processes of life share a common source would negate any sense of alienation from the land or from other peoples. While the philosophy of the unified God is one of undifferentiation, the figure of God in biblical narrative often appears as a jealous being in the sky. The character of God who motivates through fear or punishment is hard for most contemporary readers of the Bible to accept. The text of the Hebrew Bible as it has reached its contemporary readers attributes few female characteristics to the figure of God and is inherently misogynistic. Rather than attempt to reconstruct a counter-goddess tradition, we refer the reader to *The Hebrew Goddess*, a commendable scholarly work by Raphael Patai. Research and reference to ancient Goddesses is integral in understanding the biblical world. Goddesses played an important role in the beliefs of many biblical women. King Solomon is described as participating in the pagan rituals of his wives. It is hard to imagine that the biblical matriarchs accepted an exclusively male concept of God. Belief in Goddesses informs the Hebrew Bible and the God of the Hebrew Bible, at times, possesses female attributes. Achieving a more expanded view of God takes more than the changing of a pronoun. The challenge to monotheistic belief is to conceive of a God who transcends gender boundaries. Accepting that all parts lead to a whole, then God is a force of undifferentiation containing both male and female aspects.

THE TRIANGULAR COVENANT

We turn to the stories of Abraham, Isaac, and Jacob in order to illustrate the second half of the Genesis cycle. When humanity is "scattered" as a result of the Tower of Babel, the cycle drops to its nadir and the state of estrangement seems irreparable. At this point, God calls Abraham away from his home and tells him to get "on the road." Abraham's acceptance of the journey and subsequent departure begins a counter-movement in which the Genesis cycle shifts direction from estrangement to redemption.

Abraham repairs the separation caused by the building of the tower, Isaac redeems Noah's failure, and Jacob rediscovers an Edenic balance. Through this symmetry, the Genesis cycle comes full circle and reaches a point of completion. Abraham is "called out" on the journey when God says to him, "Leave your own country, your kinsmen, and your father's house, and go to a country that I will show you" (Gen. 12:1). Abraham must surrender to the unknown and depart from security to pursue a relationship with God. Abraham, on God's command, breaks from his family to adopt the life of a wanderer.

Wandering gains new meaning in the Abraham story. Where Cain's nomadic life was a sign of his curse, Abraham's journey illustrates that he is chosen. Abraham wanders in order to forge a connection with a land "promised" to his descendants. God speaks to Abraham when he is camped on mountains or in groves of trees. Each time God speaks to Abraham, it is of the land and the grandiose future which it will sustain.

During Abraham's pre-covenental wanderings, God observes his abilities and loyalties while Abraham surveys the land. Since he has left everything that is familiar, Abraham reconstructs his identity as he wanders. Abraham is not sealed in a womb-like world like Adam and Noah. Exposed to foreign peoples and rough terrain, Abraham's sense of self is constantly being altered by experience.

Said R. Isaac, "This may be compared to a man who was traveling from place to place when he saw a building in flames. Is it possible that the building lacks a person to look after it? he wondered. The owner of the building looked out and said, 'I am the owner of the building.' Similarly, because Abraham our father said, 'Is it conceivable that the world is without a guide: The Holy One blessed be He, looked out and said to him, 'I am the guide, the Sovereign of the Universe.'" Said R. Berekiah: "What did Abraham resemble? A phial of myrrh closed with a tight fitting lid and lying in a corner, so that its fragrance was disseminated. As soon as it was taken up, however, its fragrance was not disseminated, similarly, the Holy One, blessed be He, said to Abraham: 'Travel from place to place, and thy name will become great in the world.'"[16]

After Abraham has proved his fidelity by keeping on the path, God establishes a covenant with him. This covenant is triangular in structure and binds Abraham to God through the medium of the land. Abraham's acceptance of responsibility for this land is Abraham's acceptance of God. In a night-time vision, God says to him, "I am the Lord who brought you out from Ur of the Chaldees to give you this land ... know this for certain, that your descendants will be aliens living in a land that is not theirs" (Gen. 15:7-13). By connecting Abraham's life-cycle to the earth, God redeems a scattered humanity. By remaining in Canaan and using its resources responsibly, Abraham will be able to communicate with God and receive divine protection.

The irony of the covenant is that the land which Abraham is promised is not the land of his birth. It is, in fact, inhabited by other peoples. "That very day the Lord made a covenant with Abram, and he said, 'To your descendants I give this land from the River of Egypt to the Great River, the river Euphrates, the territory of the Kenites, Kenizzites, Kadmonites, Hittites, Perizzites, Rephaim, Amorites, Canaanites, Girgashites, Hivites, and Jebusites." (Gen. 15:18-21). The second ironic element of the promise of progeny is that it is followed by the information that "Abram's wife Sarai had borne him no children." Abraham's "divine mission" is inextricable from Sarah's journey cycle. Sarah must resolve her relationship with God before Abraham's quest can be fulfilled.

Despite the contradictions of the covenant, Abraham agrees to uphold it and pass the connection to God and land to his descendants. When Abraham is ninety-nine years old, God reasserts their agreement. "I will fulfill my covenant between myself and you and your descendants after you, generation after generation, an everlasting covenant, to be your God, yours and your descendants after you. As an everlasting possession I will give you and your descendants after you the land in which you are now aliens, all the land of Canaan." (Gen. 17:6-8). In this encounter with God, the covenant is reviewed and infused with more emotion. There is a sense that Abraham needs God's promise to counteract his own sense of marginalization as an alien claiming foreign land. To sustain in him the state of flux, God must assure Abraham that his wanderings are paving the way for future stability.

Abraham marks the covenant physically through the ritual of circumcision. God instructs Abraham, "You shall circumcise the flesh of your foreskin, and it shall be the sign of the covenant between us" (Gen. 17:11). Though he does not possess the land and does not have an heir, Abraham carries the promise of these things in his own body. With the act circumcision, the agreement is manifested. The covenant becomes part of Abraham's body as he is a part of the land.

The triangular covenant is made between Abraham, God, and the land of Canaan. It represents an earth-inclusive concept of the divine. In traditional thought, this covenant binds the Hebrews (Jews) to the land of Israel, but in a more universal sense, it represents the divinity involved in any human interaction with the earth. The promised land is all land.

FIRE AND THE KNIFE

Isaac is known to be the "son of his father and the father of his son," more noted for being a link in the chain of patriarchs than a character of his own. It is true that the parallel story of Rebekah is more detailed and more engaging. Her decisiveness is evident at all stages of her progression from independence to marriage to motherhood. The fact that little mention is made of Isaac's actions may be proof of his passivity.

Isaac is important in this discussion in that his ascent of Mount Moriah and confrontation with God redeems Noah's failure to enact God's agenda in the post-flood world. Isaac's right of passage and encounter with God is entwined in his father's test. Although God and Abraham have solidified their relationship with the triangular covenant, God still tests Abraham's loyalty. God commands, "Take your son Isaac, your only son, whom you love, and go to the land of Moriah. There you shall offer him as a sacrifice on one of the hills which I will show you" (Gen. 22:2). Abraham's reaction is not mentioned, only that he follows God's directions and takes his son to be sacrificed.

Isaac climbs the mountain carrying the tools of his own destruction. "So Abraham took the wood for the sacrifice and laid it on his son Isaac's shoulder; he himself carried the fire and the knife" (Gen. 22:7). Abraham leads his son to the top of the mountain where he binds him on an altar. He raises the knife to slaughter his son when an angel appears and stops him. Legend has it that Isaac was lying on his back with his eyes toward heaven. The angels of God cried out and shed tears before God. Some of the tears fell into Isaac's eyes and, for this reason, he became blind in his later years.

On the mountain, Isaac sees beyond fear. He has a vision of God as being inextricable from his own life. By following his father and making no protest to his binding, Isaac prepares to sacrifice himself and confront God. Where Noah evaded God and sought an escape from the trials of the alliance, Isaac offers his whole self. This action restores God's trust in humanity and paves the way for Jacob's reunion.

A STONE FOR A PILLOW

After Jacob tricks his father into giving him his older brother Esau's blessing, he had better get going. His brother is a hunter, a large man known for his strength and his flaming red hair. According to the law of primogeniture, the blessing belongs to Esau. Rebekah undermines the patriarchal order to fulfill a prophecy which she received during her pregnancy. She manipulates the situation to ensure that her favorite son succeeds. When Jacob voices an objection to the overthrow of the law, Rebekah accepts full responsibility for the rebellion. She tells him, "let the curse fall on me, my son, but do as I say" (Gen. 27:13).

Esau does not know of his mother's hand in the matter and pledges to kill Jacob as soon as their father has died and has been properly mourned. To save Jacob from Esau's wrath, Rebekah convinces Isaac that the time has come for Jacob to marry. She implores, "I am weary to death of Hittite women! If Jacob marries a Hittite Woman like those who live here, my life will not be worth living." Rebekah directs Isaac's decision and propels Jacob's journey. She sends Jacob to a foreign land in much the same way that God sent Abraham. Rebekah's voice leads Jacob on to the road.

As a traveler, Jacob gains a sense that God walks with him. The first night away from home, he sleeps with a stone for a pillow and dreams of a ladder on which angels drop and climb. Jacob visualizes the connection between heaven and earth. In the morning, Jacob calls to God and sets the conditions for their alliance. As God tested Abraham, Jacob tests God. He says, "if God will be with me, if He will protect me on my journey and give me food to eat and clothes to wear, and I come back safely to my father's house, then the Lord shall be my God" (Gen. 28:20-21).

At a later point in Jacob's journey, after his sons have murdered their neighbors in a blood bath of revenge, Jacob leads his entire family to the place of his dream (Bethel) and builds an altar. His description of God reveals the fulfillment of his conditions. He refers to God as the one "who answered me in the day of my distress, and who has been with me all the way that I have come (walked)" (Gen. 35:3). In addition to being with him on the roads that he travels, Jacob feels the presence of his God on the path of his life.

The breakthrough achieved in Jacob's journey is the resynthesis of humanity to the land and, therefore, to God. Jacob attests to the fact that God has been with him "all the way." Each step of Jacob's journey brings him to a greater intimacy with the invisible deity. In his dreams, Jacob moves from a position of observation (the ladder) to a dialogue (the dream in which God tells his to return home, Gen. 31:10-14) to full contact (wrestling with the angel). Where Abraham forges a contract which links him to the land, Jacob's consciousness is fused with God and the land of His promise. Jacob does not need a contract with God because the presence of God is part of his journey.

In walking "the way," Jacob achieves an Edenic balance. When Adam inhabited Eden, there was no separation between Adam's body and his environment. Adam's being, his body and mind, was part of a womb-like world designed by God. Jacob walks the land in God's company and defines himself through the journey. While he does not live in a womb-like world, Jacob still envisions himself as part of a larger system. Carrying on the traditions of his father and grandfather, he is an integral part of God's plan. Through Jacob's experiences, both physical and psychological, he realizes his connection with the divine and uses the lessons of his dreams to benefit his life. The bond with God serves him well as a traveler, a shepherd, and head of a family.

On the return to his birth-place with a large family and "two companies," Jacob has a direct encounter with God. The night before the reunion with his brother, he wakes and crosses the Jabbok tributary. Separated from his family, he meets a man with whom he wrestles until dawn. "So Jacob was left alone, and a man wrestled with him there until daybreak. When the man saw that he could not throw Jacob, he struck him in the hollow of his thigh, so that Jacob's hip was dislocated as they wrestled" (Gen. 32:25). The encounter is marked by an injury which causes Jacob to limp for the rest of his life. "The sun rose as Jacob passed through Penuel, limping because of his hip" (Gen. 32:31). In contrast to Abraham who conducts a ritual of circumcision to mark his covenant, Jacob is transformed by his brush with God. Abraham can be compared to someone who gets a tattoo to mark a passage while Jacob is altered by extreme experience. Jacob's limp is the mark of his walk in a supernatural realm. Adam's pain of labor resulted from his disobedience and subsequent estrangement; Jacob's pain becomes a sign of his choseness. By accepting pain as a component of his relationship to God, Jacob absorbs Adam's pain of separation and redeems the estrangement.

In the morning, Jacob's opponent asks to be set free. Jacob answers, "I will not let you go unless you bless me." The man responds by asking, "'What is your name?', and he answered, 'Jacob.' The man said, 'Your name shall no longer be Jacob, but Israel, because you strove with God and with men, and prevailed'" (Gen. 32:27-28).

Jacob's renaming is the second sign of his transformation. His identity is changed to include the name of God. As Jacob's name is converted to show his triumph over estrangement, Jacob renames the location of the encounter. "Jacob called the place Peniel, 'because,' he said, 'I have seen God face to face and my life is spared' (Gen. 32:31). This naming of place is part of the reconciliation of Adam's estrangement. In keeping with Abraham's covenant, God changes Jacob's name and Jacob renames the land. God is part of him and he is part of the earth. Jacob returns to the state of intimacy from which Adam departed. He makes the choice to return to his homeland in the same manner that Adam chose to upset the balance of the garden.

The Genesis cycle reaches its completion when Jacob returns to Canaan, settles the land, and founds the nation of Israel. The return to God is complete in the period of Jacob's stability. After the rotation has been completed, another begins. Joseph, Jacob's son resettles in Egypt and begins a new saga of departure, exodus, and return.

THE FEMALE BUDDY STORY

The most striking difference between the male and female journey sequences is that the male heroes must split from familial and intimate relationships to keep company with God while female heroes make their journeys in pairs or in the company of other women. Sarah's journey is linked with Hagar's. Rebekah travels with her nurse Devorah and other female "companions," and, of course, the famous sisters Rachel and Leah share the same path and the same man. We refer to these stories as well as the story of Ruth and Naomi as female "buddy stories."

In the book of Ruth, which we assert was narrated by a woman, the "buddy" relation is overt and the love shared by Naomi and Ruth comprises the primary theme. In Genesis, we learn of the existence of female relationships when these relationships reach a point of tension. This is probably because, like times of barrenness, tensions in the female community grab the attention of a male documenter. Despite the fact that the stories of Sarah and Hagar and Rachel and Leah are fraught with tension and competition, the women stay together until the shared goal of family establishment is achieved. In contrast to Abraham and Lot, Sarah and Hagar complete a journey cycle together. Finally, despite their jealousy plays, there is no decisive split between Rachel and Leah like the one between Jacob and Esau. Perhaps no love is lost between these pairs of women, but they do stay together to ensure the continuity of the female line.

VISION OF THE WILDERNESS

In the Genesis narratives, the stories of women are subsumed in the description of the male journey. While this text proposes a perspective of parallelism, not patriarchy and promotes the reconstruction of the female journey over the complaint that there is not enough female material, it is crucial to realize that female stories have been fragmented, edited, and reduced. The stories of the matriarchs are blended into the stories of their husbands. Yet women in the position of "secondary wife" or women who are not wives at all maintain a distinct identity. These women warrant separate stories because they are not Hebrews and cannot be defined in terms of Hebrew men. Hagar the Egyptian, the Queen of Sheba, and Ruth the Moabite all fit into this category. In the designation of "otherness," there is a sense of distinct origin and character. Through their very foreignness, their identity maintains a integrity of its own.

The sojourn of Hagar the Egyptian resembles the male journey sequence of departure, vision, and return more than the female model of barrenness, protest, and conception. Entwined in Sarah's struggle with barrenness, Hagar's story provides evidence of another tradition of female journey stories. When Sarah sends Hagar to sleep with Abraham in the hope of building her lineage, she seeks to undermine natural law. Hagar responds by trying to overthrow the familial order established by Sarah. "And when she knew that she was with child, she despised her mistress" (Gen. 16:4). Because Sarah has placed such great emphasis on the power of childbirth, when Hagar conceives she believes herself to have superior power.

Sarah complains about Hagar's behavior to Abraham who leaves the matter for the women's realm. "Abram replied to Sarai, 'Your slave-girl is in your hands; deal with her as you will. So Sarai ill-treated her and she ran away" (Gen. 16:6). Hagar runs to a spring of water in the wilderness where she has her first direct encounter with God.

The angel of the Lord found her by a spring of water in the wilderness on the way to Shur, and he said, 'Hagar, Sarai's slave-girl, where have you come from and where are you going? She answered, 'I am running away from Sarai my mistress.' The angel of the Lord said to her, 'Go back to your mistress and submit to her ill-treatment. The angel also said, 'I will make your descendants too many to be counted.'" (Gen. 16:7-11)

Of this encounter, Savina Teubal writes, "According to the narratives, Hagar experiences both an epiphany (manifestation) and a theophany (revelation)."[17] The structure of her vision is thus made valid.

When Hagar runs away during her pregnancy, the angel sends her back to Sarah's household to give birth to her child. Perhaps Sarah's ill-treatment is the price which Hagar must pay for pre- and post-natal care. The angel does not allow Hagar to give birth in the wilderness. If we fit this scene into a female journey model, then this is Hagar's prenatal vision. The angel guides Hagar and tells her that it is not the right time for her departure from the community. She must learn to tolerate Sarah's conditions, at least for a while.

Hagar marks her experience by naming the location of her encounter. "She called the Lord who was speaking to her by the name El-Roi, for she said, 'Have I indeed seen God and still lived after that vision?' That is why men call the well Beer-lahai-roi" (Gen. 16:13-15). Hagar returns to Sarah's household and gives birth to Ishmael. When Ishmael is grown and Sarah has given birth to Isaac, Hagar is forced to leave the household. Whether motivated by Ishmael's "laughing" at Isaac or the thought of "this slave-girl's son sharing the inheritance with my son Isaac," Sarah insists that Hagar be driven into the wilderness.

Abraham rose early in the morning, took some food and a waterskin full of water and gave it to Hagar; he set the child on her shoulder and sent her away, and she went and wandered in the wilderness of Beersheba. When the water in the skin was finished, she thrust the child under a bush, and went and sat down some way off, about two bowshots away, for she said, 'How can I watch the child die?' So she sat some way off, weeping bitterly. God heard the child crying, and the angel of God called from heaven to Hagar, 'What is the matter, Hagar? Do not be afraid: God has heard the child crying where you laid him. Get to your feet, lift the child up and hold him in your arms, because I will make of him a great nation.' Then God opened her eyes and she saw a well full of water; she went to it, filled her waterskin and gave the child a drink. God was with the child, and he grew up and lived in the wilderness of Paran. He became an archer, and his mother found him a wife from Egypt" (Gen. 21:14-21).

When Hagar's eyes are opened to the well of water, she learns to locate resources in the wilderness. She receives instruction of how to survive in the desert. Her "vision" ensures her survival.

The nature of Hagar's vision stands in direct contrast to the story of Lot's wife. Lot's wife becomes paralyzed in the desert because she cannot "raise her eyes" or look forward. Fixated on urban life, she looks backward to behold the destruction of Sodom. "But Lot's wife, behind him, looked back" (Gen. 19:26). Lot's wife lacks the ability to see beyond life in a hedonistic city; she has no "wild vision" and no name.

Hagar's vision, directed by God, is a personal evolution which allows for her survival. Lot's wife's backward glance represents what Paul Spilenger calls "the sin of backsliding." Her punishment is immobility, "and she turned to a pillar of salt" (Gen. 19:26). Spilenger cites a positive outcome of this transformation. "Lot's wife is an epitome of divine art, conveying a narrative in the form of an image ... she is a stone that speaks."[18]

The paradox of Lot's wife is that although she ceases to live, she gains immortality as a symbol. According to Spilenger, "she is also a suitable icon for the ambivalence of retrospection, the looking back that simultaneously causes death and immortality."[19] Looking to the past creates a death to the present as well as an immortality bound in memory. When the present only serves to recall what has already occurred, the symbols of the past replace the existing situation and causes the "retrospecter" to, in a sense, die.

A WATER-JAR ON HER SHOULDER

The most fascinating aspect of Rebekah's story is its beginning. Rebekah appears as a young independent woman who takes the risk of leaving home and venturing into the unknown. We follow Rebekah's journey as she matures, marries, and becomes a mother. Both Rebekah's character and her journey are developed, especially when compared with her husband Isaac of whom little is written. The qualities of hospitality and forwardness which Rebekah displays as a girl carry over into her life as a matriarch. Rebekah's actions attest to a certain degree of female autonomy in the biblical world.

The scene is set for Rebekah's journey by Abraham, now an old man, discussing his son's future with his beloved servant Eliezer. Abraham makes Eliezer swear to him that he will not allow Isaac to marry a Canaanite woman, but will find him a wife from Abraham's hometown. Inherent in this request is Abraham's desire that Isaac not blend into the neighboring culture, but maintain a separate tradition.

Abraham is also concerned with who will fill Sarah's shoes and assume the matriarchal role. As well as being from his homeland, Abraham insists that the woman consent to come with Eliezer in the same way that Abraham consented to God's direction of resettlement. When Eliezer asks, "What if the woman is unwilling to come with me to this country." Abraham responds, "if the woman is unwilling to come with you, then you will be released from your oath to me." Abraham wants a strong and autonomous women for Isaac's partner.

When Eliezer asks how he will know which woman to choose, Abraham with his usual flair for the mystic assures him that an angel will appear and provide guidance. Eliezer departs with a caravan and travels to Aram-naharim (or Haran). Typical of biblical journey stories, there is no description of the terrain between Eliezer's points of departure and arrival. We do not know how many people comprise the caravan, what route they take, or what Eliezer thinks as he travels.

When Eliezer reaches Aram-naharim, he goes to survey the women at the well. He arrives, "towards evening, the time when the women come out to draw water" (Gen. 24:11). Female assembly by water occurred during evening hours. Why evening? Perhaps to escape the heat of the day or because the day was devoted to household labor while the evening allowed for more social activities.

From the confusion over which woman to choose, we can assume that Eliezer witnesses a large assembly. Following Abraham's suggestion, the servant asks God for a sign:

> O Lord God of my master Abraham, give me good fortune this day; keep faith with my master Abraham. Here I stand by the spring, and the women of the city are coming out to draw water. Let it be like this: I shall say to a girl, 'Please lower your jar so that I may drink;' and if she answers, 'Drink, and I will water your camels also; that will be the girl whom thou dost intend for thy servant Isaac (Gen. 24:12-14).

Before Eliezer has finished his supplication, Rebekah enters his line of vision with a water-jug on her shoulder.

To assure us of her value, the male narrator asserts, "The girl was very beautiful, a virgin, who had had no intercourse with a man" (Gen. 24:16). Although her beauty is emphasized, it is through her actions that Rebekah indicates her choseness. Eliezer approaches and asks for a drink from her jug. She turns to him and without any hesitation or fear, offers him water. "Drink, sir … Now I will draw water for your camels until they have had enough" (Gen. 24:18-19). Rebekah's openness and hospitality are comparable to Abraham's when the three strangers appeared at his tent. Rebekah acts "quickly" showing that she is genuinely concerned with the stranger's comfort.

When Rebekah has finished her task, Eliezer produces gifts and asks after her identity. "Tell me, please, whose daughter you are. Is there room in your father's house for us to spend the night?" Rebekah lists her lineage and offers him an invitation into her home. "I am the daughter of Bethuel, the son of Nahor and Milcah; and we have plenty of straw and fodder and also room for you to spend the night" (Gen. 24:23-25). By bringing Eliezer into her house, Rebekah sets the process of her marriage in motion.

With a word play, the narrator illustrates another feature of the female community. Eliezer asks Rebekah if there is room in "her father's house," but Rebekah runs "to her mother's house" to relay the story. When Rebekah's trickster brother, Laban, catches sight of her new jewelry, he runs to the well and re-extends Rebekah's invitation. "Come in, sir, whom the Lord has blessed. Why stay outside? I have prepared the house, and there is room for the camels" (Gen. 24:31). The irony of Laban's invitation is that he has run to the well and claimed responsibility for the work done by Rebekah and her mother. Where Rebekah shows Eliezer her virtues, Laban reveals his ego.

Eliezer comes into the home, but will not partake of the feast until he has told his story. He narrates the promise made to Abraham, the sign delivered by God, and the actions by which Rebekah exhibited her choseness. Whether convinced by Eliezer's story or his "costly gifts," Rebekah's father and brother consent to her marriage to an unseen relative. "This is from the Lord; we can say nothing for or against. Here is Rebekah herself; take her and go" (Gen. 24:50). In this passage, it seems that Rebekah is little more than a piece of property exchanged by men. What about Abraham's stipulation that the woman consent?

The agreement between the men is celebrated with a feast. The next morning, Eliezer is anxious to return home. Rebekah's mother and brother ask that she be allowed to spend ten more days with them before departing. Eliezer objects on the grounds that he must return to Abraham. To settle the dispute, Rebekah is consulted. "They said, 'Let us call the girl and see what she says.' They called Rebekah and asked her if she would go with the man, and she said, 'Yes, I will go'" (Gen. 24: 57-59). Rebekah's mother ensures that her daughter has a forum to voice her desires. She chooses the journey. In this moment, much like Ruth's famous pledge to Naomi, Rebekah decides to abandon the life she has known and travel to an unknown place. Like Sarah, Rachel, Leah and Ruth, Rebekah splits from her past to enter the Hebraic family.

Rebekah does not go alone, but in the company of female companions. Her nurse, Devorah, as well as other women, join her in the journey. "So they let their sister Rebekah and her nurse go with Abraham's servant and his men ... then Rebekah and her companions mounted their camels at once and followed the man" (Gen. 24:59-61). This is the "buddy" aspect of Rebekah's story. Again, there is no description of travel. We do not know where the group camped, if any romance was struck between Eliezer's men and Rebekah's companions, or what passed through Rebekah's mind as she traveled away from home.

When the caravan arrives at Beer-lahai-roi (named by Hagar), Isaac and Rebekah meet.

> One evening when he had gone out into the open country hoping to meet them, he looked up and saw camels approaching. When Rebekah raised her eyes and saw Isaac, she slipped hastily from her camel, saying to the servant, 'Who is that man walking across the open toward us?' The servant answered, 'It is my master.' So she took her veil and covered herself ... Isaac conducted her into the tent and took her as his wife. So she became his wife, and he loved her and was consoled for the death of his mother (Gen. 24:63-67).

When Isaac brings Rebekah into "the tent of his mother Sarah," he accepts her as his partner as well as the matriarchal head of the family.[20] Savina Teubal interprets this as Rebekah's induction into the order of a priestess. Rebekah steps into Sarah's place and carries on the matriarchal lineage. Isaac is "consoled for the death of his mother," and Rebekah begins the matriarchal journey.

MANDRAKES OF THE FIELD

We must keep in mind that despite the title of "matriarchs," Rachel and Leah come from a polytheistic tradition. Accepting Jacob's notion of God and joining him on his journey requires a shift in belief and lifestyle for the two sisters. Like Hagar, Rebekah, and Ruth, they must break from the past and begin anew. Their perspective must be forward-looking. Despite their compliance with Jacob's beliefs, Rachel and Leah maintain a tradition of their own.

In the midst of Rachel's barrenness, she meets her sister in the fields. Leah's son Reuben has discovered "some mandrakes in the open country" and given them to his mother. The purple flowers were believed to excite passion and aid conception and the mandrake's root was said to induce visions. Rachel begs her sister for use of the plant. Leah snaps, "is it so small a thing to have taken away my husband, that you should take my son's mandrakes as well?" Rachel bargains with her sister in a manner similar to Jacob tricking his brother out of his birth-right. "Rachel said, 'very well, let him sleep with you tonight in exchange for your son's mandrakes" (Gen. 30:15). The two sisters strike a deal so that each can gain something which she desperately wants.

Leah and Rachel are bound by circumstance and lack the ability to split from the family structure as Jacob does. Where Jacob and Esau separate to keep from murdering each other, Rachel and Leah face their rivalry every day. The negotiation over the mandrakes is representative of how they must overcome their tensions in order to keep the family intact. The exchange of mandrakes and their continued dialogue proves beneficial for both women. "That night he slept with her, and God heard Leah's prayer, and she conceived and bore a sixth son ... then God thought of Rachel; he heard her prayer and gave her a child" (Gen. 30:17-23). The interaction in the field brings the desired result to both sisters.

Before making the decision to return home, Jacob consults his wives about leaving Laban's household. With one voice, Rachel and Leah consent to the journey.

> Rachel and Leah answered him, "we no longer have any part or lot in our father's house. Does he not look on us as foreigners, now that he has sold us and spent on himself the whole of the money paid for us? But all the wealth which God has saved from our father's clutches is ours and our children's" (Gen. 31:14-16).

The sisters use their statement of acquiescence as a forum to speak out against their father. Rachel and Leah want to leave their father's house to achieve greater autonomy. Letting Jacob know of their resentments, they agree to a new life.

Rachel takes the protest one step further. When she leaves her father's house, she steals his household gods. "When Laban the Aramaean had gone to shear his sheep, Rachel stole her father's household gods, and Jacob deceived Laban, keeping his departure secret" (Gen. 31:19). Ilana Pardes explains this incident, "in light of the fact that possession of the household gods could serve as the symbolic token of leadership in a given estate, what Rachel is after in this case is analogous to what Jacob cunningly wrests from his blind old father."[21]

While Jacob carries his blessing and his notion of God in his thoughts, Rachel has a need for the tangibility of the *terafim* (household gods). Jacob receives the protection of his father's God in a dream because his father has evoked God as the force behind dreams. This picture of God is beneficial to a shepherd who spends his days wandering with his flocks. Rachel knows the gods of her father, gods who perform specific roles. In *Son of Laughter*, a fictional account of Jacob's journey, Frederick Buechner elaborates on the appearance of these gods.

> They lived on a shelf in my uncle's cellar ... One of them was a bearded child in a high peaked cap. Another wore a skirt of fish scales with plump toes and a round, full belly. Another was bald and beardless. He held his member out before him in both hands. He had no eyes and only a crack in the stone for his mouth. They told my uncle many things that he lusted to know. They told him where to look for the missing goat or the strayed lamb. They told him when to plant and where in the city of Haran to buy for least and sell for most. They told him about rain.[22]

Rachel desires these gods for practical purposes and to make her new place resemble her childhood home. Like Jacob, she wants to uphold her family's traditions and hopes for supernatural guidance on her way.

When Laban catches up to Jacob in his flight, Laban insists that his gods be returned. Jacob who has no knowledge of the theft, tells Laban, "whoever is found in possession of your gods shall die for it." Rachel shows that she has been observant of her father's and her husband's tricks.

> When he came out of Leah's tent he went into Rachel's. Now she had taken the household gods and put them in the camel-bag and was sitting on them. Laban went through everything in the tent and found nothing. Rachel said to her father, "Do not take it amiss, sir, that I cannot rise in your presence: the journey of women is upon me." So for all his

search Laban did not find his household gods (Gen. 31:33-35).

With her subterfuge, Rachel indicates the female journey. She tells her father that she is on "the journey of women," or menstruating. Rachel says this to stave off her father and in doing so indicates the importance of menstruation. To a woman for whom conception is so difficult, menstruation represents an almost divine power.

Rachel makes off with the household gods. They are part of Jacob's household until after the rape of Dinah and the revenge of Simeon and Levi. After these incidents, Jacob commands his family to "rid yourselves of the foreign gods which you have among you, purify yourselves, and see that your clothes are mended" (Gen. 35:2). After the trauma in Shechem, Jacob wants to renew his family and lighten their collective weight by getting rid of the foreign gods. The time comes for a streamlining of belief. "So they handed over to Jacob all the foreign gods in their possession and the rings from their ears, and he buried them under the terebinth-tree near Shechem" (Gen. 35:4). It is interesting to note that Rachel's death scene follows the burying of the gods.

Rachel dies on the road to Ephrathah (Bethlehem). In the midst of a difficult pregnancy, she receives advice and words of support from a midwife. We can assume that her death scene occurs during a female assembly since it immediately follows the naming of her second son.

> When there was still some distance to go to Ephrathah, Rachel was in labour and her pains were severe. While her pains were upon her, the midwife said, "Do not be afraid, this another son for you." Then with her last breath, as she was dying, she named him Ben-oni, but his father called him Benjamin. So Rachel died and was buried by the side of the road to Ephrathah, that is Bethlehem (Gen. 35:16-20).

Rachel initially names her son Ben-oni (son of my sorrow) to express her physical pain. Jacob does not want the boy to have an identity based in misery, so renames him Benjamin (son of my right hand). The midwife assures Rachel that her quest to have sons has been fulfilled. Jacob makes further testament to Rachel's journey by building her a tomb. "Jacob set up a sacred pillar over her grave; it is known to this day as the Pillar of Rachel's Grave" (Gen. 35:20).

> Bearing in mind that Ephrath is Bethlehem, the location of her tomb is not without significance. This liminal locus intimates that she makes it to the threshold of the royal city but is not allowed to enter. The future Davidic dynasty does not spring from her sons, but from Judah, Leah's fourth son.[2]

Rachel's journey may end on the road, not quite in "the royal city," but her journey is picked up and fulfilled by a later traveler on the same road, Ruth the Moabite. Ruth, also a woman of another faith, walks the road to Eprath and makes it to Bethlehem. Not only does she gain entrance, but she becomes the founder of the Davidic lineage. Ruth's journey completes Rachel's and begins another cycle of the Hebraic family.

Appendix I:
Midrashic Accounts of the Edenic separation

A midrashic story charts Adam's entire growth process in the span
of a day:

> R. Hama b. Hanina said: twelve hours only was that day. The first
> hour the dust was collected. The second he was formed. The third his
> body's parts were made. The fourth he was given the soul, the fifth he
> stood upright on his legs, sixth he named all creatures, seventh he
> came to Eve, eighth they are four, ninth they were commanded, tenth
> he sinned (disobeyed), eleventh he was punished, twelfth he was
> expelled. [Yalkut Reubeni, Jerusalem (1962), 89]

In this account, Adam is acquainted with paradise in strictly physical
terms. His development in Eden occurs in twelve hours–in the span of a
day. Darkness is not part of Adam's knowledge until he is exiled.

A second story describes the despair with which Adam encounters
darkness.

> When Adam on the day of his creation saw the setting of the sun he
> said: Alas it is because I have sinned that the world around me is
> becoming dark. The universe will now become again void and without
> form–this then is the death to which I have been sentenced from
> heaven! So he sat up all night fasting and weeping and Eve was
> weeping opposite him. When however dawn broke, he said, this is the
> usual course of the world [B Abodah Zarah 8a].

In this story, Adam sees darkness as a movement toward chaos. If
the garden becomes "void and without form," then Adam's body will
follow a similar course. In this account, external darkness creates the
state of fear. When the sun rises, Adam understands the cycle of the

day and this strikes a similar balance inside him. Experience then leads him to accept darkness.

In a story of Adam outside of the garden, he uses invention to combat his fear.

> R. Levi said in the name of the son of Nezirah: that light functioned thirty six hours, twelve on the eve of the Sabbath, twelve during the night of the Sabbath, and twelve on the Sabbath. When the sun sank at the termination of the Sabbath, darkness began to set in. Adam was terrified, surely indeed the darkness shall bruise me. Shall he of whom it was written, He shall bruise thy head, now come to attack me, what did the Lord do for him? He made him find two flints which he struck against each other; light came forth and he uttered a blessing over it; hence it is written, "But the night was light about me–ba'adeni"; i.e. the night was light in my Eden (be'edni) [Gen. Rab. 11:2].

In this story, Adam's fear is eased by the discovery of secondary light. The impulse toward invention is portrayed as a post-Edenic need. In the Garden (the ideal state), no invention is necessary. In a world where darkness causes fear, invention is required to recreate a sense of balance.

Notes

All biblical verses are according to The New English Bible, Oxford University Press, except for those designated "ot" (our translation).

Chapter one: The Biblical Cycle

1. Phipps, W. E. *Assertive Biblical Women*. Greenwood Press, (Westport, CT, 1992) 15.

2. Pardes, Ilana. *Countertraditions in the Bible: A Feminist Approach*. Harvard University Press, (Cambridge, MA, 1992) 64.

3. Teubal, Savina (1). *Sarah the Priestess: The First Matriarch of Genesis.* Swallow Press, (Athens, OH, 1984) 131.

4. Teubal, Savina (2). "The Genesis Narratives: Told by Women, Written by Men?" unpublished article presented at SBL meeting, Chicago, IL, 1994.

5. Brown, Norman O. *Love's Body.* University of California Press. (Berkeley, CA, 1966) 146.

6. *Midrash Rabbah: Genesis Rabbah* (Gen. Rab.) Freedman, H. and Simon, M. eds. The Soncino Press, London, 1961.

7. Patai, Raphael. *The Hebrew Goddess.* Wayne State University Press, (Detroit, MI, 1967) 96.

8. *Genesis Rabbah,* 28:2-3

9. Gen. Rab. 36:7

10. Ibid 36:7

11. Teubal, Savina (3) *Hagar the Egyptian.* Harper and Row, (New York, NY, 1990) 23.

12. Teubal (3), 29.

13. Patai, Op. Cit., 24

14. Patai, Op. Cit., 39.

15. Frye, Northrop. *Fables of Identity: Studies in Poetic Mythology,* Harvest Books, 1966.

16. *Gen.Rab.,* 39:1-2.

17. Teubal (3), Op. Cit., Intro, XXIX.

18. Spilenger, Paul. "Dante's Arte and the Ambivalence of Retrospection," in Stanford Italian Review vol. x:2 (1992) 252.

19. Spilenger, Op. Cit., 262.

20. our translation of Genesis 24:67

21. Pardes, Op. Cit., 70.

22. Buechner, Frederick. *Son of Laughter.* Harper (San Francisco, CA, 1993) 3-4.

23. Pardes, Ilana., Op. Cit., 71-72.

CHAPTER TWO:

THE SPOKEN TEXT

I. THE FEMALE VOICE

II. THE TARGUM AND THE MIDRASH

There is ample evidence that the ancient voice of the female prophet has been silenced. But the message in those silent texts is clamoring for recognition.

–Savina Teubal

THE SPOKEN TEXT

I. THE FEMALE VOICE

Before entering the parameters of a narrative, the readers must ask themselves, who is telling us the story? This question is asked as an initiation to a level of trust solid enough to allow belief in the narrative world. If the storyteller cannot be trusted, then neither can the landscape which she evokes. If the storyteller proves to be an experienced guide, then the travels become all the more engaging.

In Dante's ventures down the abyss of Inferno and up the mountain of Purgatory, he has Virgil, the great storyteller, as his guide. Virgil, as one author of epic, gives Dante, another author of epic, access to a fantastic world of haunting and redemption. By making Virgil a character in his epic, Dante points to the role of author as guide. As a traveler and an author, Dante relies on Virgil's established knowledge to lead him through metaphysical landscapes.

As readers traveling through the landscapes of biblical narratives, we have no personified guide. We have no Virgil. There is no name which can be pointed to as a signifier of author. We can never be sure who exactly is telling us the story. Yet we can look back through centuries of editing and rewriting and imagine the story being spoken. The cadence of biblical stories, recurring formulas, and gaps in description that could be filled in by audiences point toward the oral basis of biblical narrative. The first commandment after the People of Israel's liberation from Egypt is to "tell your son" the story of freedom (Ex. 13:8). With this commandment, the passing down of stories becomes the lifeblood of Jewish tradition. With each retelling, the stories are given life and relevance to a particular time frame.

A multiplicity of voices speaks the biblical text. They tell the stories of rivalry and love, the body and the earth, survival and the relationship to the divine. The voices speak in different languages, dialects, and accents and employ a wide range of storytelling devices.

Storytelling is an activity of stillness, a night gathering which entertains and brings the community together in the dark hours. For the audience, the storyteller must create a sense of movement within stillness. The storyteller can, through rhythm and image, lead the audience into symbolic locations. To create the sense of movement, most stories describe a journey made by a hero outside of the parameters of home. Journey stories allow a sedentary audience to experience motion. In one respect, the journey story is juxtaposed to the audience's stillness. But on another level, the narrative adds dimension to the stillness as the audience makes an imaginative journey with the storyteller as the guide. The audience gains access to new frames of mind as they follow the hero through unknown landscapes while moving through corresponding locations in their own psyche. Thus the travels of a single hero provide the means for a communal journey.

Biblical stories, like folk tales, reflect the experiences of a community. As the community structure changes, so do the stories. A community storyteller would take a skeletal story familiar to the audience and embellish it with expressions and values particular to the time. Thus, the storyteller reflects the consciousness of the times while forming it. The skeletal tale is steeped in familiarity, yet the particular setting and characters reflect emergent values. The storyteller strikes the balance between concepts previously accepted and those introduced. Different storytellers weigh this balance of known and unknown according to personal beliefs as well as those of the audience. A written text freezes these beliefs on the printed page.

As the written text became more widespread, the role of author gained importance. A single person became responsible for the text and claimed to have created a particular story. Yet fiction is a process as communal as storytelling. The author reads the symbols of her world and combines her impressions with the forms of the fiction tradition. Often, authors become marketable personalities, almost texts themselves which are processed by the media and read by the public. In such cases, authorial intention becomes as important as the text itself. We can speak of the author's values and influences, her reasons for producing the text that she does. Yet, despite the celebrated figure of the author, it is through the text that we know the author as storyteller. Beyond the personality of the author, we can see how she processes the values of her time and reflects them in fiction. As a storyteller, the author is both responsible to and responsible for the perceptions of her time. Through the text, the author communicates with a larger community of readers.

The Book of Ruth stems from a female oral tradition. Evidence of its orality is provided in the existence of different Hebrew and Aramaic versions of the story, patterns which mirror other biblical stories, and the elements of orality contained within the texts themselves. We will use the term storyteller instead of author because even in its written form, the Book of Ruth maintains integrity as an oral story. The term "storyteller" emphasizes that the teller of this tale is interested in exactly that: conveying a story to the audience.

The story of Ruth bears a striking resemblance to the story of Abraham. Ruth travels from a foreign land, pledges loyalty to God (via Naomi), settles in the land of Israel, and gives birth to "a great nation" (Davidic Dynasty). Like Abraham, Ruth leaves her country, kinspeople, and family to go an unknown land. The audacity of the pioneer is evident in both stores. Into the story of migration, the storyteller of Ruth weaves themes of cultural blending and women's self-determination and makes reference to the female tradition of which she is a part. In the Book of Ruth, the journey cycle takes on a uniquely female twist.

The tradition of female assembly (or at least our ability to chart this assembly) has three manifestations in biblical stories: naming ceremonies, harvest celebrations, and water gatherings. The naming ceremony first becomes evident in the matrilineal naming speeches of Genesis. After giving birth, a woman would be surrounded by midwives, female relatives, and friends. The new mother would take the opportunity to describe her pregnancy through the name of a child and include the female community in the birth.

These exclusively female scenes give us insight into the values of the women's community. Giving birth was viewed as the manifestation of female creative power and was celebrated by naming, or the mother's expression of her conception. Midwives played in integral role in the birth process, providing medical as well as psychological guidance. The involvement of midwives is most apparent in the collective female voice which names the children.

WOMEN AND WHEAT

Another female assembly occurs toward the end of the wheat harvest. Each spring during the harvest, the majority of the male community would spend their days and nights in the fields. Days were devoted to harvesting the wheat and nights were spent on threshing floors: round, roofless structures in the fields where the wheat was processed. The men would sleep on the threshing floors because the harvested wheat needed to be guarded from thieves and because work began early in the morning. This duty became festive and the threshing floor became known as a place of feasting and open sexuality.

> That generation was steeped in immorality, used to pay harlots from the threshing-floors, as it is said, Rejoice not, O Israel, unto exaltation, like the peoples ... thou hast loved a harlot's hire upon every threshing floor (Hos. 9:1).

While the men were gone during the wheat harvest, the women would conduct their own spring rituals. The nights when the men were away provided a time for female gatherings devoted to music, dance, and storytelling. The first recorded "wheat-harvest" assembly is made by Rachel and Leah. During the wheat-harvest, Reuben comes back from "the open country" to bring mandrakes, an aphrodisiac (and according to some, psychedelic) plant, to his mother Leah. Subsequently, Rachel and Leah meet and Rachel bargains with her sister for the use of the mandrakes. The dialogue between the two sisters results in Rachel's acquisition of the mandrakes and Leah's "hiring" of her husband for an extra night. Both women conceive as a result of the bargain and celebrate the births of their children during another harvest assembly.

We suggest that the story of Ruth was part of a group of stories told during the wheat harvest assembly. The theme of famine and harvest addresses a communal anxiety and Ruth's adventures in the fields speaks to female curiosity about a male realm. The scene of Ruth going to the threshing floor at night to seduce Boaz describes a crossing of the gender barrier. This part of the story would prove particularly captivating during the harvest separation. Naomi instructs Ruth on the art of seduction:

> Now there is our kinsman Boaz; you were with his girls. Tonight he is winnowing barley at his threshing-floor. Wash and anoint yourself, put on your cloak and go down to the threshing floor, but do not make yourself known to the man until he has finished eating and drinking. But when he lies down, take note of the place where he lies. Then go in, turn back the covering at his feet and lie down. He will tell you what to do (Ruth 3:2-6).

Naomi tells Ruth to dress her best, go to the threshing-floor, and do for Boaz whatever he asks. Ruth agrees to Naomi's plan, but her acquiescence is motivated by loyalty to Naomi. Ruth reverses

Naomi's instruction and says, "I will do whatever you tell me." Ruth reminds Naomi that no man is her master and that Ruth's alliance is with Naomi. Ruth goes to the threshing-floor and does "exactly as her mother-in-law had told her."

She joins Boaz after he had "eaten and drunk" and lies down beside him "at the far end of the heap of grain." Ruth and Boaz spend the night together. In completion of the triangle of loyalty, Boaz tells Ruth, "I will do whatever you ask." Ruth rises before "one man could recognize another" so that she is not disgraced by being seen on the way back from the threshing-floor.

Ruth's descent to the threshing-floor changes her life. By going to Boaz, she begins a process of becoming a wife and a mother. We can imagine the suspense with which storytellers would describe her arrival at the threshing-floor and her seduction of Boaz. The description of decisive female action would be perfect for harvest gatherings. In the same manner that Ruth crosses political and cultural boundaries, she traverses gender boundaries to prove the flexibility of such distinctions. The story of a woman breaking through such boundaries would be an integral part of any female celebration. The fact that the story of Ruth is read today during Shavuot (Pentecost), the Jewish holiday marking the spring harvest, is evidence of the enduring tradition.

WOMEN AND WATER

The third kind of female gathering centers around bodies of water, for, in biblical times, women were responsible for its distribution. As resource managers, they would go to the well to water the flocks and bring water to the community proper. Going to the well was a group activity which insured the women's safety. Evidence of this female assembly appears in the repeated image of women gathered at the well.

Springs, fountains, ponds and wells were female symbols in archaic religions, and were often considered water-passages to the underground womb. Sacred wells especially are credited with the property of causing women to become pregnant.[1]

We have no record of how such gatherings were conducted because we view the assembly from eyes of male protagonists and narrators. But, we can use the recorded evidence as a means of reconstructing the nature of the assembly.

The first well scene appears in Genesis 24 when Eliezer, Abraham's servant, is sent to fetch a wife for Isaac from Haran, Abraham's birth-place. Eliezer, unsure of how to find the right woman, goes to the well "towards evening, the time when the women come out to draw water." He surveys the women in the hope of finding Isaac's destined bride and meets Rebekah. As well as being a place of female assembly, the well was an acceptable meeting place for young men and women. A traveler, wishing to acquaint himself with the community, would come to the well. This is the way that Rachel and Jacob meet:

> Jacob continued his journey and came to the land of the eastern tribes. There he saw a well in the open country and three flocks of sheep lying beside it, because the flocks were watered from that well. Over its mouth was a huge stone, and all the herdsmen used to gather there and roll it off the mouth of the well and water the flocks; then they would put it back in its place over the well. Rachel came up with her father's flocks, for she was a shepherdess. When Jacob saw Rachel, the daughter of Laban his mother's brother, with Laban's flock, he stepped forward, rolled the stone off the mouth of the well and watered Laban's sheep. He kissed Rachel, and was moved to tears (Gen. 29:6-12).

An exclusively female water assembly occurs when Jacob, Rachel and Leah flee Laban's household and hit the road. On the night that

Jacob wrestles with the angel, Rachel, Leah, Bilhah and Zilpah stay together on the banks of the Jabbok River. "During the night Jacob rose, took his two wives, his two slave-girls, and his eleven sons, and crossed the ford of Jabbok. He took them and sent them across the gorge with all that he had" (Gen. 32:22). While Jacob confronts his fears through a supernatural encounter, the women remain together. They probably face similar feelings of displacement and apprehension, but their manner of coping is different. Jacob goes off by himself to search out his God while Rachel and Leah keep watch over the family and comfort one another.

Female water assemblies were also conducted in Egypt. The story of Moses' life begins with the motif of women and water. To prevent her son from being murdered, Yocheved, Moses' mother, puts him in a basket and lays it "among the reeds by the bank of the Nile." Miriam then guides her brother through the water and secures his future.

> The child's sister took her stand at a distance to see what would happen to him. Pharaoh's daughter came down to bathe in the river, while her ladies-in-waiting walked along the bank. She noticed the basket among the reeds and sent her slave-girl for it. She took it from her and when she opened it, she saw the child (Ex. 2:3-7).

Miriam takes her brother to the place by the river where Pharaoh's daughter bathes. The floating baby captures the Egyptian women's attention and Miriam knows that her brother's life depends on their mercy. She watches and gauges their sympathy. When Pharaoh's daughter sees that the baby is crying, she is filled with pity. Miriam approaches, offering her mother as a wet-nurse for the baby. Pharaoh's daughter agrees to accept the child as her own. In a naming ceremony, she declares, I will call him "Moses, because I drew him out of the water."

Moses' independent journey begins when he flees Egypt after

murdering an Egyptian guard. The theme of Moses and water recurs as meets his wife, Zipporah, by a well:

> Now the priest of Midian had seven daughters. One day as Moses sat by a well, they came to draw water and filled the troughs to water their father's sheep. Some shepherds came and drove them away; but Moses got up, took the girls' part and watered their sheep himself. When the girls came back to their father Reuel, he asked, 'How is it that you are back so quickly today?' 'An Egyptian rescued us from the shepherds,' they answered; 'and he even drew water for us and watered the sheep.' 'But where is he then?' he said to his daughters. 'Why did you leave him behind? Go and invite him to eat with us.' So it came about that Moses agreed to live with the man, and he gave Moses his daughter Zipporah in marriage (Ex. 2: 16-21).

Moses' rescue of Zipporah and her sisters from "some shepherds" shows that women faced danger in the open spaces. Skeptical about meeting strange men in the desert, Zipporah and her sisters leave Moses behind. It is their father, the priest of Midian, who invites Moses into the home and family.

Miriam the Prophetess is strongly associated with water. Legend has it that a well followed the people of Israel throughout their desert wanderings. Called "Miriam's Well," it was a gift granted by God because of Miriam's merits. God made the well on the second day of the creation, and at one time it was in the possession of Abraham. It was this same well that Abraham demanded back from Abimelech, King of the Philistines. The well was shaped like a sieve-like rock, from which water would gush forth like a spout. It followed the people on all of their wanderings. Whenever they halted, it halted and settled opposite the tabernacle. When struck by the staffs of the elders, rivers would run forth and separate the different parts of the camp. These rivers caused women visiting each other to make use of ships. Upon entrance to the Holy Land, the well disappeared and was hidden in a certain spot of the Sea of Galilee. Standing upon Mt. Carmel and looking over the sea, one can notice a sieve-like rock and that is the well of Miriam.[2]

After liberation from slavery in Egypt, the people of Israel are led by Moses, Aaron, and Miriam. Moses is the prophet who speaks directly to God; Aaron mediates between Moses and the people and confronts the logistics of leadership; and Miriam is the Prophetess and leader of women. This shared role represents parallel, not patriarchal leadership. The collective effort of the siblings is chronicled in Micah 6:4: "For I brought thee up out of the land of Egypt, and redeemed thee out of the house of bondage; and I sent before thee Moses, Aaron, and Miriam." In this passage, Moses, Aaron, and Miriam are all cited as prophets. Miriam is as responsible for the liberation from Egypt as Moses. She is equally powerful in the eyes of God.

After the people of Israel cross the Red Sea, the male and female assemblies diverge. The men follow Moses as he sings a triumphant military ballad and the women "go out" with Miriam in a celebration of song and dance. Moses portrays God as an invincible and essential military ally, a figure contrary to his original vision of God: "I will ever be what I am now" (Ex. 3:14). Moses changes God's image for the newly liberated men of Israel. He describes God in military terms, hoping to capture the blood thirst of his men:

> I will sing to the Lord, for he has triumphed gloriously the horse and his rider has he hurled into the sea the Lord is my refuge and my defense, he has shown himself my deliverer ... The Lord is a warrior: the Lord is his name. The chariots of Pharaoh and his army he has cast into the sea; the flower of his officers are engulfed in the Red Sea. The watery abyss has covered them, they sank into the depths like a stone (Ex. 15:1-5).

Moses translates his notion of God into the archetypal warrior, a more marketable image. In his song, he describes the natural forces which aid the people as manifestations of this God. The fact that God can assume different forms reveals that early monotheism allowed for various depictions of the divine. While trying to wean the people from pantheism, Moses alters his understanding of God so that they will understand him.

The ally of which Moses speaks has the same name as the presence on the mountain. When Moses is alone on a desert mountain, his vision of God is of a timeless force at the core of experience. Moses comes to an understanding of God as he learns the terrain and the features of the mountain. His perception of God is based on external signs. The God understood on the top of the mountain is inextricable from the understanding of the mountain. After the people of Israel have crossed the Red Sea and seen their enemies swallowed by the same waters, God is understood as a type of sea deity responsible for the Egyptian army's demise. '

> Thou didst blow with thy blast; the sea covered them. They sank like lead in the swelling waves.Who is like thee, O Lord, among the gods? Who is like thee, majestic in holiness, worthy of awe and praise, who workest wonders? Thou didst stretch out thy right hand, earth engulfed them (Ex. 15:10-12)

Here, the presence of God is understood in terms of the wind, water, and earth which destroy Pharaoh's army. Moses interprets the splitting sea as a sign of God's strength and uses it as a device to boost his men's confidence. As former slaves, the men are unaccustomed to fighting, so Moses must provide them with self-esteem and the desire to conquer. He uses song to celebrate victory over the Egyptians and prepare his men for battles to come:

> Nations heard and trembled; agony seized the dwellers in Philistia. Then the chieftains of Edom were dismayed, trembling seized the

leaders of Moab, all the inhabitants of Canaan were in turmoil; terror and dread fell upon them (Ex. 15:14-16).

At a time of rejoicing, Moses speaks of the enemies which Israel will encounter on their quest to resettle the land. The alleged trembling of other tribes is Moses' fantasy which he transmits to his audience. In his song, God is a mighty warrior whose alliance makes the Israelites invincible. Surely if the men believe themselves to be mighty, Moses reasons, they will be mighty.

Concurrently, Miriam the Prophetess leads the women in a ritual of song and dance. "And Miriam the Prophetess, Aaron's sister, took up her tambourine, and all the women followed her, dancing to the sound of tambourines; and Miriam sang" (Ex. 15:20). The women celebrate their liberation by singing together. Where Moses narrates, Miriam engages. The ritual which she leads is interactive; gone is the space between prophet and people so profound in Moses' war ballad. Music binds the women together as they call out with a common voice. The exchange of call and response is evident in the verb *va-Ta'an* (and she answered). This verb shows that the women sang to Miriam in some form of chorus and that she responded to them with her own song. Although the dialogue is sparse, the verb *va-Taan* creates the image of a chorus in which the women sang to Miriam and were answered with a ballad paralleling Moses'. Only a brief, militaristic phrase directly quoted from Moses has survived: "Sing to the Lord for he has triumphed gloriously; the horse and his rider has he thrown into the sea" (Ex. 15:21). The extent of Miriam's song is left unrecorded.

In his study, *The Poets of the Old Testament*, Alex Gordon charts the evolution of the female chorus. "Out of the primitive communal song was evolved, in due course, the women's chorus, with its responsive reiteration of some simple theme, varied by a refrain in which the whole singing throng took part."[3] Gordon states that the differentiation of parts of a song was a direct result of the fact that the voices were different. In a similar line of reasoning, we argue that the need for a distinct female assembly emerged from the fact that women had different needs which lead to different spiritual practices.

After crossing water and arriving at a landscape of greater freedom, a tradition of female assembly begins. We can assume that Miriam's song had parallel themes to Moses'. She would have described the miracle of the splitting sea in terms of its importance to the female community. As Moses prepared the military strategy, Miriam probably outlined female roles. The power of leadership is triangulated by Moses, Aaron, and Miriam; the fiber of the community is enriched by gender specific gathering and ritual. The people cross the waters and begin their journey toward freedom as a nation, then separate so that each group can prepare themselves to come back together as a united group. Unfortunately, the integrity of Miriam's song has not been maintained, but the integrity of the tradition has.

In the Book of Judges, there is a female military ballad sung by Deborah the Prophetess, which is of comparable substance to Moses'. Legend has it that Deborah sang this victory song near Ein Harod, a spring beneath the mountains of Gilboa. Deborah sings of her own power and that of Yael, the woman who killed the fiercesome Sisera, commander of the Canaanite army.

> Mountains shook in fear before the Lord, the lord of Sinai, before the Lord, the God of Israel in the days of Jael, caravans plied no longer; men who had followed the high roads went round by devious paths. Champions there were none, none left in Israel, until I, Deborah, arose, arose, a mother in Israel (Jud. 5:5-7).

Essentially, Deborah is rapping, singing her praises to a captive audience. She is a self-described champion, a woman with confidence

enough to speak her mind. She evokes herself as a mother hearing the
voices of her daughters throughout the land. "Hark, the sound of the
players striking up in the places where the women draw water!" She
connects her individual song with other female gatherings. Deborah
imagines her voice echoed at all assemblies of women by water. She
even peers across the fence into the lives of Canaanite women.
Deborah, a woman warrior, is concerned with the sadness of the
murdered general's mother.

> The mother of Sisera peered through the lattice, through the window
> she peered and shrilly cried, "Why are his chariots so long coming?
> Why is the clatter of his chariots so long delayed?" The wisest of her
> princesses answered her, yes, she found her own answer: "They must
> be finding spoil, taking their shares, a wench to each man, two
> wenches" (Jud. 5:28-30).

Deborah's is a uniquely female ballad. Like Moses, she speaks of her
slain enemy, yet shows compassion. The Prophetess gives her enemy
a voice in the narrative history. "Enemy" personified as a concerned
mother, a symbol of benevolence. In the dialogue between Sisera's
mother and the princess, they too imagine the fates of other women.
Deborah's vision is an inward glance, mirrored in other women's
lives.

The storyteller of Ruth has knowledge of the ritual led by Miriam
the Prophetess. She connects her tale with Miriam's song through
reminiscent phrases and storytelling devices. The women of Miriam's
assembly, like Ruth and Naomi, move toward independence by
departing from the male world. The verb which describes the
women's movement with Miriam is *va-Teṣenah* (went out, f. form).
This suggests that the women separated from men and went to the
wilderness to celebrate. When Naomi leaves the fields of Moab with
her daughters-in-law, the verb *va-Teṣe* reappears. "So she went out
(*va-Teṣe*) of the place where she was, and her two daughters-in-law

with her; and they took the road to return to the land of Yehuda"
(1:7).

When Naomi and her daughters-in-law "go out" from Moab, they
leave their sickness and sorrow and move toward healing and
restoration. Their actions are self-empowering. "So with her two
daughters-in-law she left the place where she had been living, and
took the road home to Judah" (Ruth 1:8). Their "going out" is a
group endeavor. Once Naomi, Ruth and Orpah are on the road, they
can begin open communication. Like Miriam and the daughters of
Israel, Naomi and her Moabite daughters-in-law speak in call and
response. Their "song" follows a tripartite structure of supplication
and refusal.

Naomi encourages Ruth's and Orpah's departure in three speeches
of mounting passion. For Naomi's three speeches, potential converts
to Judaism are supposed to be turned away three times. The first
speech is a farewell blessing: "Go back, both of you, to your
mothers' homes. May the Lord keep faith with you, as you have kept
faith with the dead and with me; and may he grant each of you
security in the home of a new husband" (Ruth 1:8-9). Ruth and
Orpah respond with a direct protest: "We will return with you to
your own people." Naomi questions her worth and motions them
away from her. "Go back," she repeats, wishing to preserve their
innocence. "Go back, my daughters. Why should you go with me?
Am I likely to bear any more sons to be husbands for you? Go back,
my daughters, go" (Ruth 1:11-12). These words are enough to send
Orpah back to her mother's house, but do not move Ruth. Now a
two-some, Naomi and Ruth engage in a more direct dialogue.

The call and response pattern emphasizes the power equilibrium.
Instead of being talked to, the women exchange ideas in a dialogue
which allows them to be both listener and speaker. Since the role of
speaker was so often denied to women, it is emphasized in
exclusively female scenes. The coming out of Miriam and Naomi

bring them to a place of refuge where they can sound their voices and articulate their emotions. Such a separation allows them to establish their own network.

The necessity of gender specific assembly during times of transition, such as post-Red Sea crossing, has parallels in both written and implied aspects of the Book of Ruth. The story of Ruth blends scenes of men with women: Elimelech and Naomi in the fields of Moab; Ruth and Boaz on the threshing floor; with gender specific scenes: Ruth, Naomi, and Orpah on the Road to Return; Ruth, Naomi and the female chorus; Boaz and the men outside the city gates. A variety of gender combinations show the diverse aspects of life in Bethlehem. As well as being more cinematographic, the different scenes make the story more complete.

Ruth is the only biblical story in which women are the primary heroes and their world is the informing environment. The scenes of women and men are points of transition in the larger, female journey. The story begins with male death and ends with a testament to female creation. Ruth and Naomi are able to reverse fortune, counter death, and return home.

The storyteller introduces Elimelech only to show that he fled his community, brought Naomi with him, and died. His only function is to situate Naomi at her point of departure, for it is from the site of his death that she travels. Elimelech and his sons are important as catalysts who bring the heroines together. In announcing his death, the storyteller says, "And Elimelech, Naomi's husband died." Attention is called to Naomi, not the deceased. A woman is given top billing as she steps into the position of family head and the syntax of the obituary suggests that a woman is telling the story.

The detail and dialogue in the female scenes provide further evidence that the storyteller is a woman. The emotional content of Ruth's pledge to Naomi exceeds any passion shown to Boaz. The Jewish lesbian community speaks of Ruth and Naomi as a biblical example of female love. The two women care for each other first and foremost. Ruth vows her eternity to Naomi:

> When these words are read through the lens of lesbian feminist experience, they point toward something greater than a relationship of loyalty and obligation between these two women. This story of female friendship resonates powerfully with Jewish lesbians in search of role models.[4]

Their enigmatic and devoted relationship lends to the interpretation that Ruth and Naomi are lovers. They work to locate a male redeemer, but it is in the name of staying together. As they travel between the poles of life and death, Naomi and Ruth are each other's primary love. At each of these poles, men are present, but Ruth and Naomi remain attached to each other.

The story of Ruth and Naomi is a model for understanding the journeys of women in the Bible. Through the appearance of a female chorus (the women whose voices frame the tale of Naomi in Bethlehem), we discover a female oral tradition only hinted at in earlier passages. The arrival of Ruth and Naomi sends a wave of excitement through the whole city, but it is the female chorus who greets them. In a pattern of call and response, the chorus encourages Naomi to tell of her experiences. "When they arrived in Bethlehem, the whole town was in great excitement about them, and the women said, 'Can this be Naomi?'" (Ruth 1:20). The tendency in the story of Ruth is for triangular relationships. The female chorus enters with a question and fills in the role of Orpah. "Is this Naomi?" the chorus asks in the first of three identity questions in the book of Ruth. On the physical level, they are searching for familiarity. Gone for many years, Naomi has aged and is probably dressed in Moabite clothing. The chorus is looking back through the years and comparing the Naomi before them with the woman they knew in the past.

> In the past she wore a cloak of fine wool, and now she is clothed in
> rags, and you say, *Is this Naomi?* Before her countenance was ruddy
> from abundance of food and drink, and now it is sickly from hunger,
> and yet you say, *Is this Naomi?*[5]

The midrashic writers interpret this question dramatically and assume
that the question reflects Naomi's devastation. They are concerned
with Naomi's physical appearance, something which the narrator of
Ruth never mentions. Although Naomi has lost her husband, she is
not necessarily hungry, sick, or clothed in rags. The question probes
other things. Not knowing what has happened to Naomi over the
years, "Is this Naomi?" is the chorus' attempt to weave Naomi's
experience into their own. There is also an element of gossip in the
question. The women want to know where Naomi is coming from and
what she has seen. The question is also asked rhetorically as the
chorus wonders if Naomi is returning for good.

Inherent in the question is the opportunity for Naomi to take the
forum and tell her story. The women do not ask the whereabouts of
her husband and sons; they do not ask about Ruth; they ask Naomi
about her own experience. There is a tenderness in the question, a
desire to understand Naomi's situation and be sensitive to it. "Is this
Naomi?" they ask and focus entirely on her. "Who are you Naomi?"
they ask, eager for an explanation.

Naomi answers with a striking lament infused with the weariness
of travel. She responds exclusively to women as evidenced by "and
she said to them" (fem. form). She takes the women into her
confidence and without providing any details of Moab, describes her
emotional state. "Call me not Naomi (pleasantness), call me Mara
(bitterness): for it is a bitter lot that the Almighty has sent me" (Ruth
1:20). Naomi tells the women not to refer to her by her original name
which means pleasantness, but by a self-chosen name which bears the
burden of her experience. She feels that her suffering has changed her

drastically enough to warrant a new name. Naomi does not speak of any specific experience, but encodes them in her complaint against God. All of her other losses are contained in the belief that God is absent. Within her outcry against God is the Jobian aspect of criticizing the present situation in the hopes of improvement.

The chorus provides Naomi with the opportunity to externalize her grief and speak with anger about God. With this speech, Naomi ends a mourning process begun in Moab. She has reached her home as well as a place of personal resolve. The memory of her husband and sons and her sorrow will be held in the name "Mara." The female chorus ends Naomi's wandering and begins her resettlement. Among the women of Bethlehem, Naomi chooses a name to mark her transformation.

The cycle of Naomi in Bethlehem begins and ends with the voice of the female chorus. The reversal of Naomi's situation becomes evident in the contrast between the two scenes. As she selects a name, Naomi creates a new context for herself. She wraps herself in a mystique of sorrow: "I went out full, and the Lord has brought me back empty. Why do you call me Naomi? The Lord has pronounced against me; the Almighty has brought disaster on me" (1:21). Naomi left Bethlehem in a time of famine, but was "full" because she went with a husband and sons. Now, Naomi feels as barren as the fields from which she departed. The death of her family causes Naomi to belief that God is against her. Ironically, she speaks of the same God "bringing her back" and bringing her disaster.

Another parallel between the story of exodus and the story of Ruth is the renaming with the word "Mara" (bitterness). The scene which follows Miriam's song is the people's arrival at bitter waters.

So Moses brought Israel from the Sea of Suf, and they went out to the wilderness of Shur; and they marched three days in the wilderness, and found no water and when they came to Mara they could not drink of

the waters of Mara, for they were bitter: therefore the name of it was
called Mara (Ex. 15:23).

Use of the word "Mara" is a complaint against God. Verbalization of
bitterness registers an unfavorable situation and marks the desire for
change. Articulation of discontent is the first step toward alteration.

With the name Mara comes the people's fear, murmuring, and
rebellion. "And the people murmured against Moses, saying, what
shall we drink?" As former slaves, they look to a figure of authority
for guidance. The exposure of the desert weakens their faith. As a
lesson that the earth will always provide, God performs a miracle.
He instructs Moses to cast a tree in the water which makes it
drinkable and sweet. God shows the people new combinations for
nourishment and teaches them that unfavorable conditions can always
be changed. Legend has it that after this incident, Miriam's well first
appeared.

The people of Israel must learn to accept hardship as part of the
life cycle. After the springs of Mara, they come to "Elim where were
twelve springs of water, and seventy palm trees" (Ex. 15:27). Upon
leaving Elim, the people come to the wilderness of Sin and again
murmur with fear. The cycle continues and God repeatedly performs
miracles to counteract the people's disbelief. The force named as God
is the sparse land's ability to support the people. When He makes the
waters sweet, God identifies himself by saying: "I am God, your
healer" (our trans. of Ex. 15:26). God is evident in the restorative
properties of the desert.

The storyteller of Ruth seems to have knowledge of the Exodus
story. Naomi, in a similar context, uses "Mara" to name herself.
After Naomi's sojourn in the wilderness, she arrives in Bethlehem,
unsure about the future. She articulates her "bitter lot" in the hope
that it will soon change. Fear shadows Naomi's declaration. She has
reached Bethlehem, but does not know how she will support herself.

Like the newly liberated people of Israel, Naomi feels apprehensive about her return. As in the desert cycles, a renewal follows Naomi's period of disaster. Her restoration is brought about by the actions of Ruth, not by divine intervention. The "miracle" in the Book of Ruth is one of human friendship, yet the characters' transformations are as profound as the changes undergone by the people of Israel during their forty years of wandering. Naomi's waters are made sweet by the birth of Ruth's child. Naomi reappears in dialogue with the female chorus. Savina Teubal calls this scene an "example of purely female involvement. A child is born and is named by women."[6] Ironically, Ruth's voice is not heard. "Perhaps as a way of assuring the joint motherhood of Ruth and Naomi, neither of them names the child. It is the women of Bethlehem who, in a collective female voice, give him the name 'Obed.'"[7] Obed is named in a celebration of female creative power and solidarity. Although the chorus praises Ruth in the final scene, emphasis is placed on Naomi's restoration.

> Then the women said to Naomi, "Blessed be the Lord today, for he has not left you without a next-of-kin. May the dead man's name be kept alive in Israel. The child will give you new life and cherish you in your old age; for your daughter-in-law who loves you, who has proved better to you than seven sons, has borne him" (4:14-16).

When the female chorus reappears toward the end of chapter four, it is to name Ruth's child. The culmination of a tradition, "the blessing of the matriarchs does not acquire a matrilineal momentum until one reaches the Book of Ruth."[8] This scene fits into the model of postnatal assembly and functions as an appraisal of Naomi's situation. The female chorus celebrates Naomi's rebirth as much as they do Obed's birth. By reversing the diction of her previous speech, the chorus highlights Naomi's blessedness. Acknowledging God's presence, the chorus tells Naomi, "He has not left you."

Naomi is twice blessed because she has an heir as well as the alliance of Ruth who has proved "better than seven sons." Naomi claims Ruth's child as her own. "Naomi took the child and laid him in her lap and became his nurse." Naomi did not give birth to Obed and it seems impossible that she could nurse him. This birth by proxy is similar to Sarah's initial claim of Ishmael, Hagar's son, and Rachel's and Leah's acquisition of children through their maid-servants. In the sense that Ruth is the extension of Naomi, Naomi can claim ownership of the child. Naomi has assumed the role of family head whose name will be continued through Obed's birth. A child is "born to Naomi," because her name will live in Israel. The chorus signals the return of Naomi's good fortune by calling her by her original name.

IN THE WOMAN'S BIBLE

In 1895, Elizabeth Cady Stanton published *The Woman's Bible* as an extension of the Coalition Task Force on Women and Religion. Stanton's agenda was to "revise texts and chapters directly referring to women" and to confront centuries of patriarchal commentary.[9] Desiring to make women more active and critical of religious politics, her comments fuse biblical narrative with early feminist rhetoric. In the true spirit of female oral tradition, Stanton retells the story of Ruth using the Moabite woman as a symbol of female liberation. In her version, Ruth the Moabite is suspiciously suffragette.

Initially, Stanton masquerades behind a scholarly voice and refers to "tradition" which "says that the Messiah was descended from two gentile maidens, Rahab and Ruth." But once the story's momentum gets going, she does everything she can to overturn the perceptions of this tradition. Of Ruth's commitment to Naomi, Stanton explains, "Naomi had a peculiar magnetic attraction for her, a charm stronger than kindred, country, or ease."[10] Although Naomi is said to exude a certain charm, there is nothing deviant or strange in Stanton's evaluation of the relationship. She speaks of it naturally and attests to the power of female bonding. The strength of Ruth's determination becomes a paradigm of the determination necessary for turn of the century women to claim their rights.

In *The Woman's Bible,* Naomi is allotted status and property: "Naomi owned a small house, lot and spring of water on the outskirts of the town."[11] By granting Naomi land and water, Stanton provides her with a "room of her own" and frees her from poverty and male dependence. Naomi becomes self-sufficient the moment that she remedies her husband's mistake by returning home. The immediate restitution of Naomi's land changes the nature of Ruth's decision to go and glean in the fields. Instead of being a response to hunger, Ruth's desire to labor reads like a feminist manifesto. "I must not sit here with folded hands, nor spend my time in visiting neighbors nor in search of amusement, but I must go forth to work."[12] Stanton gives Ruth choices. The Moabite woman can live a frivolous or indolent life if she so desires, but selects industry. Why does she work? Because "Ruth believed in the dignity of labor and of self-support," Stanton answers. Ruth becomes an example of a woman who enters society to establish her own niche. Her work is an extension of her dignity and competence. With her words on Ruth's lips, Stanton calls women out of the home and into the workplace.

Tough as nails, sexually aggressive, and smarter than most, Ruth is as much a model for the feminist approaching the millennium as it was for women at the turn of the century. While Stanton's version with its Victorian trappings is outdated, *The Woman's Bible* sets a remarkable precedent for feminist commentary. The story of Ruth is meant for retelling, reframing, and reimagining and Ruth's words take on new power with each transmission of the story. In Stanton's time, Ruth's autonomy and labor were revered. While these virtues remain tantamount to a feminist value system, we can marvel at how Ruth overcomes gender boundaries. She is nurturing and affectionate while overturning a patriarchal order and out-smarting any potential critics. Ruth the Moabite balances several roles while being confined to none of them. Her story is a testament to autonomy.

> And he turned himself.
> She clung (LFT) to him like ivy, and he began to finger her hair.
> "Spirits have no hair," he said to her and asked, "Are you a spirit or a woman?"
> " I am a woman," she said.
> "Are you married or unmarried," he queried next.
> "I am unmarried," she responded.
> "Clean or unclean?" he asked.
> "I am clean," she answered.
> Then he asked her, "Who are you?"
> She said, "I am Ruth the Moabite."
> [Yalkut, 606]

II. THE TARGUM AND THE MIDRASH

THE MIDRASH

The Midrash is viewed as the soul of the Jewish people, a literary work able to nourish in times of calamity. Sages who discussed biblical verses and episodes used different mediums to convey their teachings to the people. Thus the sages became the poets, moralists, and teachers of their time. They gained authority not only for being eloquent in their teaching but, mainly, for ethically sustaining a landless people. The sages gained authority for being able to explain biblical verse, while grasping the consciousness of their times. Their teaching embraced four perspectives: the aesthetic, the interpretive, the moral, and the contemporary. The aesthetic aspect expands the biblical story to increase its intellectual pertinence. In the interpretive, midrashic writers try to explain the ambiguous language of the Bible by presenting a story. The moral aspect, understood as didactic and educational, deals with good and evil. The fourth aspect, the contemporary one, tackles the current issues faced by the Jews. Questions of exile, redemption, and oppression are paramount.

For many years, the Midrash was not a recognized body of literary work among scholars. This was probably the outcome of two factors. First is the focus placed on the Talmud which for centuries was the favorable text among scholars. Second is that the Midrash, a form of Rabbinic literature, was considered esoteric and a bit inaccessible. The Midrash has not been thoroughly investigated. Only recently have scholars such as Ophra Meir and David Stern focused on its stories.

Midrash Rabbah is the largest eclectic work for the Pentateuch and the five scrolls. The adjective Rabbah (large) used to describe the Midrash suggests that this work, in comparison to other midrashic work, is larger and more comprehensive. The Midrash is like a body of water with depths of interpretation and is the largest national creative work after the Bible.[13] *Midrash Ruth Rabbah* is one of the oldest midrashim, written more or less at the time of the Song of Songs. The sources of the midrash are derived from the *Jerusalem Talmud* (y. Tal.), *Genesis Rabbah* (Gen. Rab.), *Pesiqta de Rab Kahana* (Pesiq. Rab Kah), and *Leviticus Rabbah* (Lev. Rab).

Ruth Rabbah covers the biblical text and interprets the story verse by verse, for example, Elimelech's death is given a definitive cause:

Why then was Elimelech punished? Because he struck despair into the hearts of Israel. He was like a prominent man who dwelt in a certain country, and the people of that country depended on him and said that if dearth should come he could supply the whole country with food for ten years. When a dearth came, however, his maidservant went out and stood in the marketplace with her basket in hand ... He was one of the notables of his place and one of the leaders of his generation. But when the famine came he said, "Now all Israel will come knocking at my door, each one with his basket." He therefore arose and fled from them.[14]

Naomi is viewed in the Midrash as a woman "whose actions were fitting and pleasant." In order to illustrate her character, the midrashic storyteller compares her past status with the manner in which she returns.

> In the past she used to go in a litter, and now she walks barefoot, and you say: 'Is this Naomi? In the past she wore a cloak of fine wool and now she is clothed in rags, and you say; Is this Naomi? Before her countenance was ruddy from abundance of food and drink, and now it is sickly from hunger, and yet you say: Is this Naomi?'[15]

In the Midrash, Ruth's pledge of commitment to Naomi becomes on oath of conversion.

> She said to her, "Do not sin against me; do not turn your misfortunes away from me; I am fully resolved to become converted under any circumstances, but it is better that it should be at your hands than at those of another."[16]

According to this version, Naomi is the means of Ruth's conversion. If Naomi denied Ruth her faith, it would be perceived as a sin. Ruth gains stature in the midrashic story, where she is famous for being David's mother.

> R. Abbahu said: 'If a giant marries a giantess, What do they produce? Mighty men. Boaz married Ruth. Whom did they produce? David, of whom it is said, skillful in playing, and a mighty man of valour, and a man of war' (I Samuel 16:18).[17]

The Midrash uses hyperbole to answer riddle. Its rhythm is call and response, a cadence of oral tradition. The Midrash reflects oral tradition by recording what people are thinking about and what their values are. The story is changed to be attractive and pertinent to a new generation of audiences.

THE TARGUM

The Aramaic Targum of the story of Ruth (Tg. Rut.) was written in the Aramaic dialect of the West. In many ways, this Targum is an expansion and adaptation of the early Targum of Johnathan. At certain times in Jewish history, the people could not read or understand biblical texts. To transmit the legacy, translators would stand up in public places and tell the story. "So they read in the book in the law of God distinctly, and gave the sense and caused them to understand the reading" (Neh. 8:8). These storytellers combined old stories with contemporary consciousness to create prophecy. The language of these prophets was Aramaic, the lingua franca of exiled Jews. Their stories are more than translations, for they present interpretations of laws, creeds, and beliefs. Gradually, the Aramaic versions were written down: the translation of the Torah is a final product of the first century CE, the final translation of the Prophets is a product of the fourth century CE, and the final translation of the Hagiographa is a product of the ninth century CE. The Aramaic storyteller, like the midrashic one, was extremely interested in filling in the biblical story's gaps. The story was expanded to fit the times.

A substantial number of the exiles who returned to Jerusalem were not Hebrew speaking people. Their language, Aramaic, gradually became the language of the synagogue. In the 8th century, the time of King Hezekiah, emissaries said to Rab Shakeh, representative of the King of Assyria: "Speak, I pray thee, to thy servants Aramean language for we understand it. Talk not with us in the language of Judah" (II Kings 18:26).

In its form, the Aramaic Targum includes interpretations of the laws, remnants of moral preaching, and religious philosophy. On certain points, the Targum and the Midrash cross over, indicating communication between the two texts. About the first line of the book of Ruth, the Aramaic storyteller says:

> In the days when the judges judged, there was a great famine in the land of Israel. Ten great famines were decreed by heaven to come upon the world from the day of creation until the coming of the King. The Messiah will reprove them with living on Earth ... The tenth famine will be in the future not a famine for bread, nor a thirst for water, but to hear the words of God.[18]

This expansion resembles the midrashic one, as both texts were informed by the same biblical source. We suggest that the rabbinical teaching on the Targum of Ruth either came to us in the Aramaic version, or was translated from the Hebrew to the common people. The Aramaic version of the story of Ruth is clearly midrashic and retold to enforce new perceptions. According to E. Levine, the targum confirms the tradition of Shavuot and contains some moderate but old *halakhot* as evidenced in the translation of 4:5.

> *Va'amar Boaz b'yom zabintakh yet haqla ... hayav at lemifroq uva'ei l yabbama ... la'aqama sum mita 'al ahsanteh.* And Boaz said, the day you acquire the field from the hand of Naomi and from the hand of Ruth the Moabitess you must acquire her by the levirate and marry her, so the name of the deceased will be preserved and called upon his inheritance.[19]

Echoing the story of Tamar, the story of Ruth calls levirate marriage laws into question. In the case of the death of a brother, the Targum recommends the following: "*Dilma lehon attun metinan 'ad di yirbun keitata denatra leyabbam.* Would you wait for them until they matured, as a woman watches over a young levir to marry her."[20]

The Midrash on Ruth contains many haggadic components which are also found in the *Jerusalem (Palestinian) Talmud, Pesiqta de Rab kahana, Leviticus Rabbah,* and *Genesis Rabbah.* This Midrash presents exegesis of the biblical story verse by verse, often departing from the text and navigating a strange course. In the attempt to suggest the story's date, the midrash says:

> In the days when the judges judged, Woe unto that generation which judges its judges, and woe unto the generation whose judges are in need of being judged! As it is said, and yet they hearkened not unto their judges (Jud. 2:17).

Who were the judges? Rab said: They were Barak and Deborah; R. Joshua b. Levi said: They were Shamgar and Ehud; R. Hanna said: They were Deborah, Barak, and Jael. The word "judge" implies one, "judges" implies two, "the judges" three.[21]

From four words, the sages present two teachings. The first one is their moral perception, supported by the biblical verse of Jud. 2:17 and the second is their attempt to fix the historical date of the events. Their interpretation spins from the grammatical structure of *S'fot haSoftim* which includes the infinitive construct *S'fot* and the noun *Softim* with the article *he*, the, in its plural form. The attempt to fix the historical date is argued by three different sages Rab,[22] R. Joshua b. Levi,[23] and R. Huna.[24] In contrast to these perceptions, we find that Josephus dates the story in the time of Eli: "Eli the high priest was governor of the Israelites. Under him, when the country was afflicted with a famine."[25] The Targum suggests that it was in the time of Ibzan, the judge who is mentioned in Jud. 12:8. Yet Jewish tradition holds the idea that the book of Ruth was written down by the prophet Samuel.[26] In Yalkut Shimoni, we find the following:

> And there was a famine in the land, a parable, A province that owed

arrears to the king, who sent a tax collector to collect it. What did the people of the province do? They assaulted him and insulted him ... It was in the days when the judges judged. If a person of Israel was found worshiping idols and a judge wanted to pass a sentence on him, the worshiper would come and flog the judge saying, "what he wanted to do to me, I have done to him."[27]

This story accentuates the moral perception of the sages as we have mentioned above. The midrashic storyteller, on the other hand, offers another interpretation of *Vayyehi* as conveyed by R. Hiyya Rabbah:[28] "Whenever it is said, 'And it came to pass' (*Vayyehi*), it may denote either trouble or joy; if trouble, unprecedented trouble, if joy, unprecedented joy."[29] The midrashic storyteller in Yalkut ends his story of the tax-collector with "woe to the generation that judged its judges."[30] In other midrashic versions, we find the following: "Woe unto that generation which judged its judges, and woe to the generation whose judges are in need of being judged! As it is said; and yet they hearkened not unto their judges" (Jud. 2:17).[31] The moral teaching of the midrashic passage echoes the biblical statement, "and they would not hearken unto their judges, but they went whoring after other gods and bowed themselves unto them" (Jud. 2:17). The concept appears again in Yalkut 598, "woe to the generation whose judges are in need of being judged." However, this statement is connected to the fact that Elimelech left *Eretz Yisrael* because of the famine. The midrash struggles to understand Elimelech's punishment: "But it has been taught: In time of pestilence gather in your feet, and in time of famine, spread out your feet."[32] Ruth Rabbah teaches: "In times of pestilence and times of war, gather in thy feet. Gather your feet means to stay at home while spread out your feet means to go to another place."[33] Why, then, was Elimelech punished? The midrashic storyteller suggests that he struck despair in the heart of his generation and embellishes the fact that Elimelech was one of the leaders of his generation. The Targum storyteller refers to Elimelech as *Nefaq gavra (rabbah) min bet lehem,* a great man went out of Bethlehem. Both post-biblical storytellers emphasize Elimelech's prominence to accentuate their opposition to his flight. Moreover, the Aramaic storyteller kept his perception of Elimelech as a *Gavra Rabbah,* great man, by making him a military tribune in the Moabite army (*vehavo taman rofilin*). The Aramaic storyteller used the same noun derived from the Latin noun *rufuli,* a military tribune, high official, to translate Est. 9:6 *Vehovidu hamesh me'ah guvrin kulhon rofilin mi-devet Amaleq,* and they killed five hundred men, all of them military tribunes (high officials) from the house of Amaleq.[34] The midrashic storyteller is looking for justification of the punishment. While telling the biblical story, he assumes a more assertive language.

In the Bible, Elimelech's resettlement is described as follows: "They arrived in the Moabite country and there they stayed" (Ruth 1:2). In the midrash, it appears as: "At first they came to the cities, but they found the inhabitants steeped in transgression. They then went to the large cities and found a dearth of water. They thereupon returned to the cities."[35] The storyteller of the midrash suggests that *Va-yih-yu-sam* means they had already been there.

The non-canonical storytellers are as interested in asserting their own moral and philosophical perceptions as they are in clarifying the biblical story. From the verse, "and Elimelech, Naomi's husband died," the midrashic storyteller contemplates on a statement made by R. Johanan, "All must die" (b. Ber. 17a) and says:

All must die and death must come to all.
Happy then that man who departs from this world with a good name.
The death of a man is felt by none but his wife.[36]

In this version, Elimelech is called "Naomi's husband" because his death impacts her more than anyone. In the teaching of R. Jose b. Halafta, we find the following:[37]

> Never during my life did I call my wife 'my wife,' or my home, 'my home,' but I called my wife 'my home' and my home 'my wife.' Nor did I call my ox 'my ox' or my fields 'my fields,' but I called my ox 'my fields' and my fields 'my ox.'[38]

Elimelech associates his wife with his home and his ox with his fields. R. Jose's teaching sheds light on the sages' perception of women. A woman is to the home as the ox is to the fields, the medium through which nourishment and comfort is given. Without the woman or the ox, the home and the fields are unyielding. It is as if in his last moments, Elimelech comes to terms with his own blindness. Once Elimelech dies, the midrash reduces Naomi to a woman of little importance. R. Hanina says:[39] "And she was left, and her two sons, R. Hanina, the son of R. Abbahu said: 'She became like the remnants of the meal-offerings.'"[40] In contrast to the midrashic storyteller, the Aramaic storyteller describes the condition of Naomi and her sons in a sparse and straightforward manner. Her vulnerability is emphasized: "And Elimelech, Naomi's husband died and she remained a widow and her two sons orphans."[41] The Aramaic storyteller continues his description of the social situation, implying that the two sons without the instruction of their father, did not follow the law. Without paternal guidance, the sons transgress. The vav conjunction implies a generational continuum: "And her two orphan sons disobeyed the command of the Lord and they took wives from the daughters of Moab, one named Orpah and the second Ruth (the daughter of Eglon, king of Moab) and they dwelt there about ten years."[42] The storyteller conveys the events and hints that the sons deviated because they did not have a paternal figure. What was the "command of the Lord" that they transgressed? Was the law of

Deuteronomy "an Ammonite or Moabite shall not enter into the congregation of the Lord" (Deut. 23:3) known by Elimelech's sons? The Aramaic storyteller believes so. In another interpretation, there is an attempt to relate the deaths of the two sons to their delay in returning to the land of Israel. Thus their sin was in remaining there "about ten years." In this same interpretation, Mahlon and Chilion marry Ruth and Orpah, daughters of Eglon, King of Moab to gain standing and esteem.[43] Of the phrase, "and they took them wives," the midrash says: "It was taught in the name of R. Meir: They neither proselytized them, nor gave them ritual immersion, nor had the new law Ammonite, but not Ammonitess, Moabite, but not Moabitess been propounded that they should escape punishment on its account" (Ruth Rab 2:9).[44] In other sources, we find that Elimelech's sons did not convert their wives before or after marriage and this was their primary mistake. On the verse, "and the Lord said unto me, Distress not the Moabites" (Deut. 2:9), we read the following:

> And what was forbidden to Moses was forbidden to them, and also because the precious pearls have not yet issued from them. For Ruth was in the days of the Judges. She was the daughter of Eglon, King of Moab, and when Eglon was killed by Ehud they appointed another king, and his daughter was left in the charge of a guardian. When Elimelech came to the field of Moab, Ruth married his son. She was not made a Jewess by Elimelech, but she learnt all the ways of his house, and the rules about food, and when she went with Naomi, then she was converted.[45]

However, this belief is not widespread. In other teachings, it is suggested that Ruth and Orpah converted before marriage. As soon as Orpah's husband died, she returned to worshiping other gods. It seems that the sage wanted to emphasize the shallowness of her conversion. The image of Ruth and Orpah as proselytes is enforced by *Lekah Tob* through a pun. The storyteller suggests a reading of the verb *Še-nit-ya-ha-du*, having a private union between them, as meaning to become a member of the Jewish faith. Thus love-making served as the Moabite women's conversion.[46]

To emphasize the male voice in the story of Ruth, the sages question Ruth's determination to be a Jewess. The midrash reminds us that the law requires a person who desires to convert be refused. If he returns and requests again, he must be refused. Only on his third petition, may his desire be acceded:[47] "R. Samuel b. Nahmani said in the name of R. Judah b. Hanina, Three times it is written here 'turn back,' corresponding to the three times that a would-be proselyte is refused, but if he persists after that he is accepted."[48] Ruth persists in spite of Naomi's discouragement. She commands Naomi, "Do not urge me to go back and desert you" (Ruth 1:16). Here, the midrashic storyteller asserts: "When Naomi heard this, she began to unfold to her the laws of conversion, saying: 'My daughter, it is not the custom of daughters of Israel to frequent Gentile theaters and circuses ... it is not the custom of daughters of Israel to dwell in a house which has no mezuzah.'"[49] Naomi intercepts Ruth's surrender by setting down conditions. Since Naomi does not say this to Ruth in the original story, we can assume that it is the midrashic voice of prohibition. The male writers tell their audience how to behave like a daughter of Israel.

POST-BIBLICAL NOMENCLATURE

The sages read Elimelech as Elai *melekh*, "to me shall the kingdom come." Naomi is read as, *Ne'imah*, sweet or pleasant. Although she later changes it to Mara, bitterness, Naomi reappears sweetened by the end of the story. In *Yalkut*, we find a whole lineage:

And the name of the man was Elimelech, said R. Hanan b. Rabbah, said Rav, Elimelech, Salmon, Ploni Almoni (such a one), and Naomi's father, all of them were sons of Nahshon the son of Amminadab. And what does it mean? That even the one who has the merit of his forefathers, nothing will stand for him when he went out to a foreign land.[50]

Of Mahlon and Chilion it is said:

And why are they called Mahlon and Chilion? Mahlon, because they pretended to be sick. Chilion, because they deserve extinction.[51]

About Orpah's fate, they write:

And Orpah kissed her mother-in-law, but Ruth clave unto her. Let the sons of the kiss (the one who kissed) fall in the hand of one who clave as it is written: These four were born to the giant (ha-ra-fah) in Gath, and fell by the hand of David. Raba (fourth generation of Amoraim in Bablylonia) taught because of the four tears Orpah shed on her mother-in-law, she was worthy of four mighty men who will come forth out of her offspring.[52]

Yet another teaching by R. Isaac suggests that the four giants were Orpah's reward for walking with Naomi for four miles.[53]

The Aramaic storyteller attributes the death of Mahlon and Chilion to their marriage with foreigners and residence in an unclean land. Staying true to the biblical story, he adds some of his sociopolitical and religious views: "And since they disobeyed God's word and married foreign people, their days were cut off and both of them Mahlon and Chilion died in the unclean land and the woman remained bereaved of her two sons and a widow of her husband."[54] Of Naomi's "rising up," the Aramaic storyteller says:

And she rose up, she and her daughter-in-law and returned from the field of Moab because she was informed in the field of Moab by the word of mouth of a messenger that the Lord remembered his people and gave them bread for the merit of Ibzan, the leader, and his prayer which he prayed before God, he is Boaz the pious.[55]

The Aramaic storyteller adds components to Ruth's and Boaz's meeting:

> God will repay you very well in this world because you acted kindly
> and your perfect reward for the world to come is before the Lord God
> of Israel that you come to convert and to be converted. May you be
> covered by the shade of his divine presence and saved from Gehinam
> and may your share be with Sarah, Rebecca, Rachel, and Leah.[56]

Three components are given by the Aramaic storyteller: acts of kindness, ability to change, matriarchal behaviour. Such characteristics mirror the values as well as the religious precepts of the storyteller's time which were rewarded in the world to come. "If thou hast studied much of the Law much reward will be given thee, and faithful is thy taskmaster who shall pay thee the reward of thy labour, and know that the recompense of the reward of the righteous is for the time to come."[57] The storyteller adds a very interesting component. Ruth's conversion and her dwelling under the wings of the divine presence save her from Gehinam and give her a share among the matriarchs.

The Aramaic storyteller, like the biblical one, suggests a continuity between Ruth and the matriarchs. The noun *Hulqakh* in Aramaic pl. *Hulqaya, Hulaqin* translates into a share or portion and implies a share in a whole. The Aramaic storyteller refers to all four matriarchs, where the biblical storyteller only speaks of Ruth being "like Rachel and Leah" (4:11). As Rachel and Leah built the house of Israel, Ruth builds the house of David.

The midrashic storyteller searches for clues to Ruth's appearance. "R. Johanan (second generation in Palestine) said: Whoever saw her was sexually excited."[58] Boaz is immediately taken with her, "when he saw how attractive she was and how modest her attitude, he began to inquire concerning her."[59] R. Samuel Uceda expands this perception:

> Behold, Boaz came from Bethlehem and saw such a beautiful woman in the field that anyone who saw her immediately became sexually excited ... He said to the reapers 'the Lord be with you, to save you from the evil inclination and will not forsaken you in his hands to seduce you to look at this woman.' They told him; 'the Lord bless thee, because you need this blessing too.'[60]

All Ruth's actions are depicted by the storyteller as being very kind and gentle. Her extraordinary virtue is passed on to David.

> Who are the twenty-two righteous women? They are those whom Solomon praised in the case of 'who can find a virtuous woman?' (Prov. 31:10) ... Many daughters have done virtuously (31:29), this is Ruth who was worthy that David and his upright sons came forth from her. R. Johanan said: Why Ruth? Because from her came forth David who satiated the Holy One, blessed be He with songs and praise.[61]

First and foremost on the midrashic list of importance is Boaz, the righteous man. He is not only a very wealthy man, but a man who has vision, a man of the law and, according to the Aramaic storyteller, "a hero who is powerful in the law." In the Midrash, Boaz becomes the main character around whom the plot is woven. Boaz becomes the agent of miracle:

> Resh Lakish said: Ruth was forty years of age and had not yet been vouchsafed children as long as she was married to Mahlon. But as soon as that righteous man prayed for her, she was vouchsafed as it is said: blessed be thou of the Lord, my daughter.[62]

Midrashic storytellers also heighten the religious tone. Of Naomi's first taste of the crops of Bethlehem, they write: "She did eat in this world, she sufficed for the coming days of the Messiah and she left for the world to come."[63] The Targum, as well as midrashic literature, reflects a teaching relating to the reading of the scroll of Ruth during the feast of weeks, Pentecost. In many places, we find the Targum speaks of Boaz as a member of the court or a learned person while in the Midrash, he is depicted as one who decreed certain laws and customs. His tone is quite a bit more self-assured and pompous:

> Boaz said in reply, "I commanded concerning you, he commanded only in response to the males. And it has been prophetically told to me that from you there will arise kings and prophets, because of the kindness that you did for your mother-in-law."[64]

In another verse, when Naomi instructs Ruth what to do on the threshing-floor, she hints at Boaz's importance by stating: "and you shall ask guidance of him, and he will tell you, according to his wisdom, what you should do."[65] The most explicit attempt at Boaz's valorization is when he is cast as a Sanhedrin: "And Boaz went to the gate of the court of the Sanhedrin, and he sat there with the elders. And lo, the redeemer whom Boaz had mentioned to Ruth passed by. So he said, 'come over and sit here man of modest deportment.'"[66] Indeed, the mention of "Sanhedrin" corresponds with the status of Boaz as a member of the Sanhedrin. While the anachronism is obvious, it is presented anyway. The storytellers of the Midrash and the Targum made an extreme effort to bring the story as close as possible to the realm of male understanding. They were intent on bringing their time into the biblical story and bringing the biblical story into their time. Writers of the Midrash and Targum took the story, inserted new laws and opinions, and brought it from a female domain into a male one.

In another place, the Targum makes some references to the *Taryag Mitsvot*: when Ruth proclaimed her desire to follow her mother-in-law, Naomi responded: "we are commanded to observe the Sabbath and Holy Days, not to walk more than two thousand cubits." When Ruth says "where you stay, I will stay," the Targum has Naomi say: "we are commanded to observe six hundred and thirteen commandments."[67] The idea of the *Tehum Shabbat*, Shabbat limit, is found for the first time in the Mishnah: "If a man went out (beyond the Sabbath limit) on a permissible errand and it was then told him that the act had been done already, he has the right to move within two thousand cubits in any direction."[68] The *Taryag Mitsvot*, the six hundred and thirteen commandments are mentioned in tractate Makkot. R. Simlai taught that the *Taryag Mitsvot* were given to Moses.[69] From the above sources, it is very likely that the writers of the Targum are interested in asserting the values of their time.

In the Targum, Boaz gives a lengthy sermon to Ruth on the threshing floor about his power and the Lord's commandments:

> And now, daughter, have no fear. I will do for you everything you request. Because all of those who sit at the gate, the great Sanhedrin of my people, know that you are a righteous woman, and you have the strength to bear the Yoke of the Lord's commandments.[70]

The language is anachronistic, but the same point gets across. Ruth is the paradigm of a righteous woman; she can be invoked by Sanhedrin and old men at the gate as well as midwives and women by the well. Ruth, famous for infiltrating the male power structure, is praised in a male domain. She is spoken of in the story's dialogue and in midrashic assembly. The praise of the Midrash differs from that in the Bible. Likewise, the praise bestowed on Ruth by later female commentators has a tone more applicable to our times. Ruth, the female hero, was often cast into a role of submission by the rabbis and writers of midrash. These bonds were unfettered by women scholars who approached the text and created their own commentary. The gates of biblical criticism, so long sealed to women, opened.

Midrash is an ongoing project of observing ancient texts and fusing their lessons with contemporary ones. The Bible is built of questions. The questions invite response and dialogue between person and text. By being observed, a story takes on new dimensions. Midrash serves as a mirror of how audiences frame biblical stories. It is a dynamic process of considering and reconsidering. Midrash always changes, while the Bible remains the same. The enduring stories usually explain us better than we explain them. So we talk about them, reformulate our ideas, take a look at ourselves. The myths resonate in our psyche and generate our dreams.

Appendix II:
The Other Voices
Decies repetita placebit. (Horatious, De arte poetica)

In their search for explanation of the punishment inflicted on Elimelech and his sons, the writers of the Midrash drew on an analogy from Job. According to their study, the punishment was not inflicted upon them at once, but gradually. Both midrashic storytellers (*Midrash Ruth Rabbah* and *Yalkut Shimoni*) present a lengthy teaching. Before God punishes a person, He deprives him of his property, his household, and his family. After such losses, the person is punished directly. The writers of the Midrash present their case in the following matter:

In the story of Job we read: "There came a messenger and said, the oxen were plowing ..." (1:4). "There came also another one and said the fire of God ..." (1:6). Then the Chaldeans fell upon the camels, then the servants were slain, and then Job became bereaved of his sons and daughters. In the minds of the midrashic storytellers, the following idea is strongly endorsed: "The merciful One never enacts retribution of man's life to begin with."[1] So from the analogy in the case of Job, the midrashic storytellers suggest that this Jobian motif can be seen here too: "And so it was with Mahlon and Chilion also, First of all their horses, their asses and their camels dies, then Elimelech, and lastly the two sons. And the woman was left."[2] When the Aramaic storyteller tells his story about the death of Naomi's two sons, he maintains that everything that happened to them was a result of leaving their land, marrying foreigners, and dwelling in an unclean place. Unlike the midrashic storytellers who drew their analogy from the fate of Job, the Aramaic storyteller stayed close to the biblical story and added some of his sociopolitical and religious views: "And since they disobeyed the command of God's word and married foreign people, their days (life) were cut off and both of them, Mahlon and Chilion died in the unclean land and the woman remained (bereaved) of her sons and (a widow) of her husband."[3] In his presentation of the social condition of Naomi, the Aramaic storyteller already mentioned her social condition in V.3. However, the fact that Naomi is a bereaved mother as well as a widow is emphasized. The Aramaic storyteller seeks to accentuate Naomi's loneliness and vulnerability.

The biblical storyteller in her presentation of Naomi's reaction to her new social condition says: "Then she rose with her two daughters-in-law that she might return from the country of Moab, for she had heard in the country of Moab how the Lord had visited his people in giving them bread" (1:6). The Aramaic storyteller expands this verse by adding some information which is not found in the biblical story.

And she rose up, she and her daughter-in-law and returned from the field of Moab because she was informed in the field of Moab by the words of the mouth of a messenger, for the Lord remembered his people, the house of Israel to give them bread for the merit of Ibzan the leader and his prayer which he prayed before God, he is Boaz the pious.[4]

Among the additional components that the storyteller adds, we find the following: Up to this moment, Naomi was very passive. Now she takes charge of her own life. The storyteller accentuates her determination to go back to her own land. Now that she remained by herself, a widow and a bereaved mother, she is depicted as one who is trying to make her life better. Yet while the biblical storyteller conveys that "she had heard" without giving any details or saying how she heard of the good tidings, the Aramaic storyteller tells us that a messenger or an angel of God was the harbinger of good fortune. The midrashic storyteller, on the other hand, suggests that Naomi heard the good tidings from "peddlers making their rounds from city to city."[5] Yet, when the midrashic storyteller discusses the second half of the biblical verse "And they went on the way to return to the land of Judah" (1:7), he said: "They transgressed the letter of the Law and journeyed on the Festival, Another interpretation of 'And they went ...' is that the way was hard for them ... discussing the laws of proselytes."[6] Does R. Johanan who presented such a teaching have a basis for his description of Naomi's journey? Indeed, one can argue that since Ruth and Naomi arrived in Bethlehem "in the beginning of the barley harvest" (1:22), that they may have departed during the Passover festival. However, we would like to suggest that R. Johanan does not accuse Naomi of any transgression. On the contrary, by stating that their journey began on the Festival, he praises her for her determination to leave the fields of Moab and return home.

Moreover, let us pay attention to the statement: "discussing the laws of proselytes." Surely he deduced this teaching from the verb *Va-te-lakh-na* and they went, of the root *HLKh,* from which the noun *Ha-la-kha,* law or tradition is also derived. "They two went" (1:19)–Is it possible that the biblical storyteller seeks to evoke the binding of Isaac? The midrashic storyteller views it in the following way: "So they two went. R. Abahu said: Come and see how precious in the eye of the Holy One blessed be He, are the converts. Once she decided to become converted, Scripture ranks her equally with Naomi as it says: 'So they went until they came to Bethlehem.'"[7] The midrashic storyteller is interested in giving the story an expression of religious reality, in which the divine intermingles with the human. In that sense, the midrashic storyteller strives to read a dialogue between heaven and earth in the biblical text.

Of the book of Ruth, Rudolf Alexander Schroeder stated, "no other poet in the world has written a more beautiful short story."[8] It is a story of well executed subplots which introduces the mother of the Davidic Dynasty as an outsider and wanderer. Even more shocking, Ruth is from Moab, a people born from an incestuous union between a father and his daughters. Despite her origin, Rabbinic literature claims that Ruth did not die until she saw her descendent, King Solomon sitting on the throne and judging the case of the harlots.[9] Moreover, the Messianic line is supposed to stem from the House of David.

From the patriarchal lineage, the Davidic dynasty stems from Boaz who is a descendent of Judah and Tamar (Gen. 38). Again we encounter an incestuous relationship between a father and his daughters-in-law. The midrash also describes Boaz: "And Boaz and his court arose and instituted that greetings should be by the name of God."[10] In the Midrash, Boaz has the ability to see into the future: "I was told in a prophecy that from you will come forth kings and prophets, because of the kindness you have done with your mother-in-law."[11] Moreover, Boaz is said to be a member of the Sanhedrin; "And Boaz went to the gate of the court of the Sanhedrin and he sat there with the elders."[12]

Ruth's personal history is also enlarged by the midrashic writers:

> She was the daughter of Eglon, king of Moab, and when Eglon was killed by Ehud, they appointed another king, and his daughter was left in the charge of a guardian. When Elimelech came to the fields of Moab, she was married to his son. She was not made a Jewess by Elimelech, but she learnt all the ways of his house, and the rules about food, and when she went with Naomi, then she was converted.[13]

Thus, in Rabbinic literature, Ruth redeems her ancestors. At this point, Jewish tradition paved the way for the two descendants of incestuous relationships to become the founders of the Davidic dynasty. Christianity which often follows the path of Judaism claims that Jesus' lineage is from the house of David. Messianism is born from incest.

For Jews, the Messiah who has not yet come will restore justice to the world and allow for supernatural events to occur.[14] Rabbinic literature sets different periods for the arrival of the Messiah. In this literature, the coming Messiah stands at the center of many discussions. He is the one to initiate changes in the life of the people. In this literature, we find a strong definition marking the difference between the Messianic era and the world to come. The Messianic era is the time when humanity will leave behind animal impulses and become perfectly moral beings. The world to come, in many ways, is viewed as a popularization of the ideal future. Dealing with the Messiah and clearing the way for the Davidic dynasty, the Midrash says: "Naomi said to her: My daughter, whatever good deeds and righteous actions you are able to acquire, acquire in this world, for in the world to come; 'Death shall part thee and me.'"[15]

About Ruth's and Boaz's night on the threshing floor, the Midrash says:

And it came to pass at midnight that the man was startled and he might easily have cursed her, but God put it in his heart to bless her, as it is said: Blessed be thou of the Lord my daughter. And he turned himself. She clung to him like ivy and he began to finger her hair. Spirits have no hair, he thought, and he said: Who art thou?[16]

The biblical storyteller restrained herself from a graphic description of what happened that night on the threshing floor, especially when Boaz tells Ruth to "Tarry this night." Li-ni, the verb meaning to stay overnight, to lodge. The LXX translate *aulisteti,* which has the same meaning as the Hebrew, so translates the Aramaic storyteller. In Rabbinic literature, we find the following statement: "This night you will spend without a husband, but you will not be without a husband for another night."[17]

The dialogue is further reconstructed:

And he turned himself. She clung (LFT) to him like ivy, and he began to finger her hair.

"Spirits have no hair," he said to her and asked, "Are you a spirit or a woman?"

" I am a woman," she said.

"Are you married or unmarried," he queried next.

"I am unmarried," she responded.

"Clean or unclean?" he asked.

"I am clean," she answered.

Then he asked her, "Who are you?"

She said, "I am Ruth the Moabite."[18]

The nouns, *Shif-hah* and *Amah* are synonyms which mean handmaid or servant, but can also mean concubine. In conversation, it was used as a token of humility. Thus, when the biblical storyteller tells us that Ruth says, "may I ask you a favour not to treat me only as one of your slave-girls," according to the Midrash, she is saying, "I will not be your mistress, but I am your handmaid." They also read an offer of marriage in her statement: "Spread therefore thy skirt over thine handmaid" (3:9). According to them, Ruth says: "Let your name be called upon your handmaid by having me as your wife, since you are the redeemer."[19] Another voice intones moral superiority in Ruth's manner of request: "R. Berekiah said: Cursed be the wicked: Elsewhere it is said: She caught him by his garment, saying: 'Lie with me' (Gen. 39:12), but here she said: 'Spread therefore thy skirt over thy handmaid.'"[20] Boaz responds: "Blessed be thou of the Lord my daughter for thou hast showed more kindness in the later end than at the beginning" (3:10). What was Ruth's first kindness? What was her later kindness? While there is no way to point out the later kindness, the Targum suggests that Ruth behaved exactly as a woman who is awaiting the levirate marriage: she did not go "whoring after young men." From this we can deduce that Ruth's later kindness was her revealing Boaz's "feet." Boaz responds by saying, "As the Lord livith lay down until the morning." Why did Boaz need to take an oath? The Midrash has a ready suggestion:

> She is unmarried and you are unmarried. You are looking for a wife and she is looking for a husband. Thus, arise and have intercourse with her and betroth her. And he took an oath to his evil inclination (not to touch her) and to the woman he said, 'lay down until the morning.'[21]

On Ruth's return to her mother's house, Naomi asks her, "Who art thou my daughter?" The midrashic authors probe this question for other meanings: "Did she then not recognize her? Yes. But she meant; 'Are you still a virgin (pe-nu-yah, unmarried) or a married woman?' She answered: 'A virgin': And she told her all that the man had done to her."[22]

Whether the story of Ruth involves historical dates or not, it does present a glimpse of life in a farming society. The storyteller presents the vitality of the women in this society by making them the active force in the story and by giving them voices. For this reason, we identify the voice behind the story as a woman's.

Notes

Chapter two: The Spoken Text

1. Teubal (3), Op. Cit., 25.

2. Ginzberg, L. *Legends of the Bible.* Jewish Publication Society (Philadelphia, PA, 1956) 369-372.

3. Gordon, A.R. *The Poets of the Old Testament.* Hodder and Stoughton (1912) 23.

4. Alpert, R. "Finding Our Past: A Lesbian Interpretation of the Book of Ruth" in *Reading Ruth* Kates, J.A. and Twersky Reimer G., Ballantine Books (NY, 1994) 91-97.

5. Ruth Rab. 3:6.

6. Teubal (2), Op. Cit., 9.
7. Pardes, I. Op. Cit., 106.
8. Pardes, I. Op. Cit., 170.
9. Stanton, Elizabeth Cady. *The Woman's Bible.* Coalition Task Force on Women and Religion (Seattle, 1981) 9.
10. Stanton, E.C. Op. Cit., 37.
11. Stanton, E.C. Op. Cit., 39.
12. Stanton, E.C. Op. Cit., 39.
13. Bialik, H. N. *Devarim Be'al-Peh (Heb),* 44.
14. Ruth Rab. 1:4.
15. Ruth Rab. 3:6.
16. Ruth Rab. 2:22.
17. Ruth Rab. 4:5.
18. Tg. Ruth 1:1.
19. Tg. Ruth 4:5.
20. Tg. Ruth 1:3.
21. Ruth Rab. 1:1.
22. Abbu Arikhc, 1st generation–Babylonia, 5th, C.
23. 1st generation Palestine.
24. 2nd generation Babylonia.
25. Josephus, Ant. 9.3.18.
26. B B. Bat 14b.
27. Yalkut, Ruth 596.
28. The 1st generation of Amora'im in Palestine, a disciple of Rabbi BHul. 141a-b we find the following: "any Baroitha not edited by R. Hiyya or R. Oshaia is erroneous."
29. Ruth Rab. Proem 7.
30. Yalkut, Op. Cit.
31. Ruth Rab. 1:1. See also *Leqah Tob L'Megilat Ruth.* S. Bamberger (ed.) 1887.
32. Yalkut, 598.
33. Ruth Rab. 1:4.
34. See also B B. Nes 49b, 107b.
35. Ruth Rab 2:6.
36. Ruth Rab. 2:7.

37. 3rd generation of Tana'im, considered to be the author of tractate kelim. cf. Mkelim 30:4. For more information see; Bassfrued, T. "Zur Reaction der Mischna," *Monatsschrift fur Geschicte und Wissenschaft das Judentums* (MGWJ 1907), 427 ff.

38. Ruth Rab. 2:8.

39. 4th generation of the Amora'im in Palestine, see Y Pesah 3:7.

40. Ruth Rab. 2:8.

41. Tg. Ruth 1:3.

42. Tg. Ruth 1:4.

43. See Iggeret Shemuel for Ruth 1:5.

44. Ruth Rab. 2:9. For the question of Immersion, see b. Yebam. 46 a-b, Bker. 8b-9a.

45. Zohar, Balak 190a.

46. The pun is *Še-nit-ya-ha-du,* changing the *ha* to read *Še-nit-ya-ha-du.*

47. Leqah Tob, Tosephta, (supp.) 48-49.

48. Ruth Rab. 2:16. Samuel b. Nahmani is of the 3rd generation in Palestine. Judah b. Hanina is of the 1st generation in Palestine.

49. Ruth Rab. 2:22-23.

50. Yalkut Ruth, 599.

51. Yalkut Ruth, 596.

52. Yalkut Ruth 599. Rabba is of the 4th generation of Amora'im in Babylonia.

53. Ibid.

54. Tg. Ruth 1:5.

55. Tg. Ruth 1:6.

56. Tg. Ruth 2:12.

57. M Aboth 2:16.

58. Ruth Rab. 4:5.

59. Ruth Rab. 4:6.

60. Iggeret Shemuel for Ruth 2:4.

61. Midrash ha-Gadol (MHG) Gen. 373. See also B B. Bat. 14b. R. Johanan is of the second generation in Palestine.

62. Ruth Rab. 6:2; Yalkut Ruth 606.

63. Yalkut Ruth 603.

64. Tg. Ruth 2:11.

65. Tg. Ruth 3:4.
66. Tg. Ruth 4:1.
67. Tg. Ruth 1:16.
68. M. Erub. 4:3-6 cf.; 13 Erub 48.b, 51 a-b; PErub 3:4, 19.
69. B Makk 23b.
70. Tg. Ruth 3:11.

Appendix Notes: 1. Ruth Rab. 2:10. Also Yalkut 695. 2. Ruth Rab. 2:10. 3. Tg. Ruth 1:5. 4. Tg. Ruth 1:10. 5. Ruth Rab. 2:11. 6. Ruth Rab 2:12, Yalkut 601. 7. Yalkut, 601, Ruth Rab. 3:5. 8. See Lamparter, Helmut. 9. Ruth Rab. 2:2, B.Bat 91b. 10. Ruth Rab 4:5. 11. Tg. Ruth 2:11. 12. Tg. Ruth 4:1. 13. Zohar, Balaq 190a. 14. See Derekh Eretz Zut, ch. 1. 15. Ruth Rab. 2:24; see also B Sabb. 63a. 16. Ruth Rab. 6:1. 17. Ruth Rab 6:4. 18. Yalkut, 606. 19. Tg. Ruth 3:9. 20. Ruth Rab. 6:2. R. Berekia is of the 4th generation in Palestine. 21. Yalkut, 606, see also Ruth Rab. 6:4. 22. Ruth Rab. 7:4.

CHAPTER THREE:

A CANONIZED TALE

If the modern historian may be allowed to wander occasionally outside of the received text.

—Elizabeth Cady Stanton

SHE CAME TO HIM WITH RIDDLES

The Queen of Sheba crossed the desert
in search of Solomon
to test him with her riddles

After many days of hot winds
she reached Jerusalem
on camels heavy with spices, gold, and precious stones
and set before him 700 riddles

Each night they would lie side by side
passing a riddle back and forth
between them

Solomon received all of her stories
witholding nothing
he gave her all dimensions of his heart

The Queen of Sheba saw all of Solomon's wisdom
and the house he had built
until she could not imagine her spirit
outside it

Over fire she told him
    "True are things I heard of you in my land
    I believed not the words until I came and opened my eyes
    Yet I was not told the half of it
    you are more than I imagined"

Solomon received more from the Queen of Sheba
than he had ever received before
or would ever receive again

He gave her all that she desired
and all that she asked
Until the morning she turned
    homeward
and faced again the desert–RSH

The same story can often be populated by different casts of characters. In this sense, the Bible is a drama of ongoing themes. The story of Sarah is similar to the story of Ruth which shares many similarities with the Queen of Sheba's story. All these women star as archetypes of strong women.

The Book of Ruth does not begin in a concrete time period. The narrator evades such specifics to avoid the story being frozen in a historical framework. Instead, the setting is the fluid time of the journey. From the opening words, time is used as a device to create a symbolic order specific to the story. The first word *va-Yehee* (and it was) is the biblical convention comparable to "once upon a time." *Va-Yehee* is repeated in two linked statements which seem to perform the function of establishing setting and situation, yet actually elude any definitive description of place or time. "And it was in the days when the judges judged and there (it) was famine in the land." This opening formula does provide more information than "once upon a time." Where "once upon a time" allows a tale to transcend any time constraint, "the days of judges judging" locates the story in a specific social climate. Because no singular judge is named, the time is characterized, but not made historical.

Perhaps the lack of a specific judge's name implies that in the period of the story, no competent individual had risen up and assumed leadership. We can surmise that "the days of judges judging" refers to a premonarchical time when the tribal system was still in effect. The repetition of the root "to judge" (*shfot ha-Shoftim*) is another device which serves to obscure the activities of this period. The age of judges is referenced as a period of chaos predating the centralization of the tribes during which "every man did that which was right in his own eyes" (Jud. 21:25).

Midrashic authors characterize this era as a time of schism and fragment.

The land of Israel was divided up at the time, and they became unduly absorbed in the division. Israel were all occupied with their tasks. One was occupied with his field, the other with his vineyard, yet another with his olive trees and a fourth with quarrying stones.[1]

The different tribes had each claimed a region and created a distinct lifestyle. The people identified themselves in terms of their tribe rather than as Israelites. Certain tribes competed with each other for resources, for power, and for alliances with neighboring peoples. With the two opening lines of the Book of Ruth, the narrator implies that this tribal period was a time of confusion and anarchy.

There are several reasons why the narrator would choose such a tactic. As a rhetorical device, the narrator may be using the repetition of *va-Yehee* to mystify time and draw the listeners into the universality of the story's theme. The "days of judges judging" is not important in terms of history, but because it creates a precarious situation in the lives of the characters. The political situation directly effects a family from a farming town. The narrator draws us away from historical concerns and into the lives of people. In an essay suggesting that the book of Ruth was written by Tamar, the daughter of King David, Adrian Bledstein writes: "The book of Ruth stands alone against the period of Judges as a humane tale of death, grieving, friendship, healing, rejuvenation, and continuation of life in a community."[2] The story stands out as a tale about the everyday realities of Israelite life. The shift of emphasis from political and military intrigues to the experience of two women is a clear indicator that the narrator is a woman.

The opening also has hints of propaganda as the period of the judges is associated with a famine. If we assume that the story of Ruth was written down during a monarchical period, then the association of the judges with disaster is a subtle technique to advocate centralization. The opening lines imply a cause and effect relationship: because there was political chaos, a famine spread through the land. By suggesting the ineffectiveness of the judges, the narrator indicates the superiority of a unified and centrally organized government. She evokes famine to contrast it with the stability and wealth of her time.

The narrator may have another agenda. By remembering the past as a time of chaos and confusion, she may be speaking against nostalgic tendencies and the maintenance of outdated prohibitions. By placing innovation (like that of the monarchy's centralization) in a positive light, the narrator prepares the audience to accept Ruth's breaking of taboos and her untraditional actions. Perhaps, as a woman, the storyteller has been denied knowledge of what "judging" actually entailed. She chooses to depict what life during this period meant for her female protagonists. She skirts over the issue of history to hasten the introduction of Ruth and Naomi. The beginning of the story serves as an indicator that the book of Ruth is a departure from the male concerns which comprise the majority of the Hebrew Bible and an entrance into the women's realm.

Despite the narrator's deliberate vagueness, the date of composition is commonly called into question. We believe that the story was told orally through centuries and the date of its conversion from a poetic oral form to a novella probably occurred during the reign of Solomon. Other scholarship suggests that the book was composed during the Persian period as a polemic against the objection of Ezra and Nehemiah to intermarriage. The thematic relationship between the Book of Ruth and the Book of Judith composed during this period furthers this thesis. Yet B.M. Vallas contradicts it:

> A book which was written in those troubled times of Ezra and Nehemiah as a protest against those men could not possess that beautiful atmosphere and those idyllic surroundings which, so skillfully, the author of Ruth creates, nor could it be possible to possess an unforced, serene and calm tone of style.[3]

Other scholars claim that the story presents an early dispute between the house of David and the house of Saul or, Gibeah, the city of Saul's origin vs. Bethlehem, the city of David's. Gibeah was the center of Saul's monarchy also known because it was the place where the Benjaminites committed a brutal rape of the concubine (Judges 19-21). Bethlehem is portrayed as an idyllic farming society in contrast to the more savage city of Gibeah. We accept that the genealogy at the end of the story was a construct added later to connect the story to the house of David. Accordingly, there are some suggestions as to where the "original" story of Ruth ended. Erich Zenger suggests the following verse as the ending: "And Naomi took the child and laid it in her bosom and became nurse unto it" (4:16).[4] His suggestion is in contrast to what Josephus writes:

> I was therefore obliged to relate this history to Ruth, because I had a mind to demonstrate the power of God, who, without difficulty, can raise those that are of ordinary parentage to dignity and splendor to which who advanced David, though he were born of such mean parents.[5]

In this case, the nature of Bethlehem is as important in characterizing the Davidic line as the characters of Ruth and Boaz. That the genealogy may have been added later, shows the importance of the connection between David's monarchy and an agrarian society. This story describing King David's humble beginnings may have been used to bolster support for the monarchy in the countryside. The genealogy adds a regal dimension to the story of Ruth's redemption by linking her bold actions with David's monarchy. The origin of Israel's centralized government is attributed to a well-structured farming community.

Robert Hubbard explores various theses regarding the Book of Ruth's composition as well as the arguments for a pre- and post-exilic date of composition. He concludes that "the earliest possible date would be after David became King of Israel (ca. 1000 B.C.)."[6] He goes on to say that "a clear recent trend now favors a pre-exilic date over the once popular post-exilic one. While opinions vary widely, the most sizable consensus favors composition during the reign of Solomon."[7] We support a date of composition during Solomon's monarchy. From the opening of the story with its emphasis on the chaos preceding centralization to the ending which asserts David's lineage, the Book of Ruth shares several themes with I Kings, the book chronicling Solomon's reign.

In the time of Judges, Israel was divided along tribal lines which often led to intense factionalism. Under the tribal system, differences were accentuated while common history and belief were de-emphasized. The people were "unduly absorbed in the division."[8] Militarily, this weakened Israel in the face of enemies as well as increasing the Israelites susceptibility to foreign influences. The monarchy of David provided an umbrella government for the various tribes, but not until the reign of Solomon were the tribal alliances dissolved and transformed into a nation. Solomon divided the country into districts and created a political as well as a spiritual center in Jerusalem. The establishment of a capital in Jerusalem represented a new era in Israelite history because it was a symbol of tribal cohesion as well as a focal point for religious practice. Jerusalem became a symbol of a revived nation. Since Jerusalem had never belonged to any tribe, no group could claim that the establishment of the capital gave them supremacy. "Lying between Judah and Benjamin, it provided a site immune from tribal jealousies."[9] Formerly a Hittite city, it was a neutral spot outside of any tribal jurisdiction. The establishment of Jerusalem transformed the people of Israel into the nation of Israel and the city later became the symbol of the people themselves.

I Kings, the Book which chronicles Solomon's monarchy, begins with a story of David approaching his death. The book begins by stating "King David was old." An old king means a weak kingdom. Just as "King David was old, advanced in years: and they covered him with clothes, but he could not become warm," the government of Israel is in a state of flux and impending instability. David's loose assemblage of the states is comparable to the clothes laid on David himself; they cover but do not provide ample protection. David's old age signals a need for change, for a new governmental order, and for a new vision of the state.

David's attendants suggest that a young virgin will be able to warm the sick king. They conduct a biblical beauty pageant similar to the one described in the Book of Esther in which the country's most beautiful virgins are lined up to be selected for royal service. David's advisors pick Abishag the Shunammite from the crowd and bring her to the palace to heal what ails David. The narrators are explicit in saying that although Abishag attended and ministered to the King, he "had no intercourse with her." This point is emphasized to show that David, known for his sexual prowess, is not the man he used to be.

As forecasted by Nathan the prophet, David's family was cursed by "never hav(ing) rest from the sword." The house of David is characterized by internal upheaval and insurrections lead by his sons. When David's son Adonijah learns of his father's deterioration, he claims the throne. The narrator gives a clue about Adonijah's character and the reason for such behavior: "never in his life had his father corrected him or asked why he behaved as he did" (I Kings 1:6). Before David has even died, Adonijah holds a self-sponsored victory feast and invites: "all his royal brothers and all those officers of the household who were of the tribe of Judah. But he did not invite Nathan the prophet, Benaiah and the bodyguard, or Solomon his brother" (I Kings 1:10).

This feast is enough to launch Nathan the prophet into a state of anxiety regarding his political future. He runs to Bathsheba, Solomon's mother, to alert her to the situation and to elicit her support. Nathan assures Bathsheba that he is concerned with her "safety and for the safety of (her) son Solomon" as he schools her in the actions which she must take. In his instruction, Nathan goes so far as to put the words into Bathsheba's mouth:

> Go in and see King David and say to him, 'Did not your majesty swear to me, your servant, that my son Solomon should succeed you as king; that it was he who should sit on your throne? Why then has Adonijah become king?' (I Kings 1:13-14)

In case Bathsheba has any doubts regarding her ability to persuade her husband, Nathan promises her that while she is speaking with David, he "will follow (her) in and tell the whole story."

Although Bathsheba is Queen, she takes a risk by going into David's chamber without being invited. She has not been summoned by the King, and he is being attended to by a young virgin. Bathsheba must approach David diplomatically and secure the throne for her son. The future stability of the entire country lies in her ability to remind David of his promise that Solomon would inherit the throne. David has not taken any action against Adonijah. Either he does not know about his son's activities or he is too dormant to crush a rebellion. By approaching David, Bathsheba operates as a political advisor, a role she has not before assumed.

Nathan's instructions to Bathsheba of how to restore order in the country are similar to Naomi's advice to Ruth of how to seduce Boaz and redeem the family. Both Bathsheba and Ruth become entwined in conspiracies and are propelled to action by backstage players. Nathan proves more anxious and assertive than Naomi and does not put faith in Bathsheba's abilities. A certain irony exists in Bathsheba's rescuing the country from political chaos. As a woman who has been repeatedly rewarded for passivity, she takes bold and decisive action by confronting the King. This scene represents a role reversal

between David and Bathsheba. When David first beheld her bathing
on her roof, he sent officers to order her to appear before him.
Bathsheba was then commanded to have intercourse with him
although she was "still being purified after her period" (2 Samuel
11:4).[10] She was rewarded for pleasing David by being made Queen.
I Kings casts Bathsheba in a very different role. She is depicted as an
older, wiser queen who approaches the king, briefs him on the state
of his own kingdom, and proves his most competent advisor.

The scene of Nathan and Bathsheba entering the palace reads like
a parody of court politics. Bathsheba goes into David's private
chamber where the aged king is being waited on by Abishag. David
regards Bathsheba and demands, "What do you want?" Bathsheba
informs him of Adonijah's insurrection. She urges him to take
immediate action because "all Israel is looking to you to announce
who is to succeed you on the throne." On a personal level, Bathsheba
compels David to act by saying that if he allows Adonijah to
continue, "my son Solomon and I shall be treated as criminals."
While Bathsheba is still speaking to David, Nathan rushes in and
interrupts the Queen. With a particular emphasis on his own political
future, he reiterates exactly what Bathsheba has said:

> He (Adonijah) has today gone down and sacrificed great numbers of
> oxen, buffaloes, and sheep, and has invited to the feast all the king's
> sons, Joab the commander-in-chief, and Abiathar the priest; and at this
> very moment they are eating and drinking in his presence and shouting,
> "Long live King Adonijah!" But he has not invited me your servant,
> Zadok the priest, Benaiah son of Jehoiada, or your servant Solomon.
> Has this been done by your majesty's authority, while we your servants
> have not been told who should succeed you on the throne? (I Kings
> 1:25-27).

In this scene, Nathan bears a remarkable resemblance to Polonious in
his over lengthy "brevity is the soul of wit" speech.

What majesty should be, what duty is, Why day is day, night night,
and time is time, were nothing but to waste night, day, and time.
Therefore, since brevity is the soul of wit, and tediousness the limbs
and outward flourishes, I will be brief. Your noble son is mad.[11]

Both Nathan and Polonious take it upon themselves to school the King
and Queen on how to handle irreverent sons while trying to
manipulate the situation to their own political advantage. The portraits
of Nathan and Polonious are humorous in their excess of words and
worries. In both cases, the narrator parodies the figure of the
self-motivated advisor and the influence that ego has in court
decisions.

David cuts off Nathan by demanding that he "call Bathsheba." As
the Queen stands before him, David swears to her that Solomon will
sit on the throne. Bathsheba, like Ruth when she first encounters
Boaz, bows to the king and says, "May my lord King David live
forever!" In this moment, great affection is shared by David and
Bathsheba. It is as if all the tensions of the court are resolved by their
dialogue. The King and Queen become allies in the truest sense. They
are equals securing a place for their son in the country's future; their
agreement ushers in Israel's golden age.

As David's death day draws near, he bestows the monarchy to
Solomon with these words: "I go the way of all the earth: be strong,
and show yourself a man" (I Kings 2:3). Solomon fills his father's
place as monarch and is "firmly established on the throne." From the
outset, emphasis is placed on Solomon's secure reign and
competence. A sense of legitimacy by both birth and ability is integral
to his agenda. His kingdom is "firmly established" in contrast to the
reigns of Saul and David and antithetical to the time of the judges.
Solomon unifies the tribes, establishes a nation as well as a national
identity, and creates a spiritual center in Jerusalem.

Solomon represents the monarch of a golden age who creates a nation while redefining the people's perception and relationship with their God. A political innovator, he forever transforms the structure of the Jewish state. First and foremost, Solomon geographically centralized the government:

> Through strict administration, a state monopoly in trade, a forced-labor policy, and political marriages, Solomon brought peace, wealth, and glory to the monarchy. The kingdom was divided into twelve administrative districts, sometimes deliberately divergent from the older tribal divisions.[12]

I Kings emphasizes the unification through the recurring motif that Solomon is king over **all** of Israel. After Solomon cleans house of Adonijah's supporters, the narrator says that Solomon's "royal power was securely established" (2:46). After he deciphers the problem of the two women who claim the same child, "they all (Israel) stood in awe of him; for they saw that he had the wisdom of God within him to administer justice." In contrast to the days of judges judging, Solomon makes decisive judgment admired throughout the kingdom. The narrator again asserts that "King Solomon reigned over Israel" (4:1). The theme of transforming the scattered tribes of Israel into the nation of Israel runs parallel to the restoration of a fragmented family which comprises the central movement in the Book of Ruth.

In chapter four of I Kings, there is a description of life during Solomon's reign which shows the complete reversal of the situations described in the first two lines of the book of Ruth. The contrast between Solomon's time and the time of the judges is made explicitly:

> The people of Judah and Israel were countless as the sands of the sea; they ate and they drank, and enjoyed life. Solomon ruled over all the kingdoms from the river Euphrates to Philistia and as far as the frontier of Egypt; they paid tribute and were subject to him all his life (I Kings 4:20-21).

This description stands in contrast to the chaos and famine during the time of the judges, and the order of events is switched. The people are well fed, content, and "all the kingdoms" are united under Solomon. The narrator of Ruth may have this description in mind as she speaks of the famine during the time of the judges. In both descriptions, the livelihood of the people is portrayed as dependent on the effectiveness of the leadership. Thus the monarchy is effective where the judges are not. The famine in *Ruth* is the polar opposite to the abundance and leisure prevalent during Solomon's reign. "All through his reign Judah and Israel continued at peace, every man under his own vine and fig-tree, from Dan to Beersheba" (4:25-26).

Since the Israelites are free from the threat of invasion, a cultural and intellectual enlightenment flourishes. Solomon becomes known not for military dexterity, but for his wisdom.

> He uttered three thousand proverbs, and his songs numbered a thousand and five. He discoursed of trees, from the cedar of Lebanon down to the marjoram that grows out of the wall, of beast and birds, of reptiles and fishes. Men of all races came to listen to the wisdom of Solomon, and from all the kings of the earth who had heard of his wisdom he received gifts (4:32-34).

Integral to Solomon's enlightenment is a sense of beauty and justice based on the natural world. Solomon spreads the concept that human life exists within natural cycles. Trees become a part of his discourse as he places a value on nature comparable to that of human life. Solomon's ecologically oriented speeches echo the words of his father who, while dying, told his son, "I go the way of all the earth."

In I Kings, a change occurs in the portrayal of women. Female assertiveness is exhibited as an attribute and not a failing. From the first scene, women take part in palace politics and play a significant role in Solomon's ability to forge alliances and create a strong monarchy. The independence displayed by women characters in the book chronicling Solomon's monarchy is another indicator that the book of Ruth was written down by one of Solomon's court scribes. In Ecclesiastes, a work often attributed to Solomon, the narrator says, "I acquired singers, men and women" (Ec. 2:8). These court singers were responsible for orally maintaining the national canon of stories and perhaps for committing these works to writing. We suggest that it was one of Solomon's singers/scribes who transcribed the popular harvest story of Ruth from the female oral tradition to the canon.

It was the agenda of such a scribe to bring women's stories into the forefront and include them in the literature of the enlightenment. Scholar S.D. Goitein proposed that the book of Ruth was composed by a "wise old woman."[13] That she was wise, we have no doubt, but we see no reason why Goitein proposes that she was old. Raised among women's stories, she would have extensive knowledge of the oral tradition. Knowing that Solomon (the great lover of women) would permit the inclusion of female stories, the scribe connected the monarchy to the pastoral tale with the closing lineage.

> This is the genealogy of Perez: Perez was the father of Hezron, Hezron of Ram, Ram of Amminadab, Amminadab of Nashon, Nashon of Salmon, Salmon of Boaz, Boaz of Obed, Obed of Jesse, and Jesse of David (Ruth 4:18-22).

With the lineage, the scribe associated the monarchy with Bethlehem and Solomon's cultural enlightenment with the acceptance of female autonomy.

The themes of intermarriage, harvest cycles, and family restoration central in The Book of Ruth have distinct parallels in I Kings.

> Solomon put all these objects in their places; so great was the quantity of bronze used in their making that the weight of it was beyond all reckoning. He made also all the furnishings for the house of the Lord: the golden altar and the golden table upon which was set the Bread of

the Presence; the lamp-stands of red gold, five on the right side and five on the left side of the inner shrine; the flowers, lamps, and tongs, of gold; the cups, snuffers, tossing-bowls, saucers, and firepans, of red gold; and the panels for the doors of the inner sanctuary, the Most Holy Place, and for the doors of the house, of gold (I Kings 7:47-50).

The temple is as much a testament to Solomon's wealth and power as it is to his God. Since Solomon was young, David assigned the task to him and told all the people, "my son Solomon is the one chosen by God, Solomon alone, a boy of tender years; and this is a great work, for it is a palace not for man but for the Lord God" (I Chronicles 29:1). There is tremendous expectation on the part of the people that Solomon build a fabulous temple and establish new forms of worship.

Solomon wants to create a permanent place to house the Ark of the Covenant so that a sense of permanence will carry over to the Israelites. The temple becomes the symbol of stability in the people's relationship to God and the stability of Solomon's kingdom. Raising the temple is Solomon's greatest endeavor. In his dedication, he makes a public address to God,

O Lord who hast set the sun in heaven, but hast chosen to dwell in thick darkness, here have I built thee a lofty house, a habitation for thee to occupy forever (I Kings 8:13).

As God set the sun in heaven, Solomon constructs the glorious city. He assures God and the listening elders that the period of wandering is over. The temple serves as a herald of a new age.

As Solomon redefines God's "dwelling place," he also outlines new parameters for the national religion. In his dedication of the temple, he asks God to act toward the people with forgiveness, acceptance, and balanced judgment. By articulating these values, he advises the people to behave in a similar manner. The requests which Solomon makes in his speech have direct thematic parallels in the book of Ruth.

Solomon holds God to the promise made to Noah that "while the earth lasts seedtime and harvest shall never cease" (Genesis 8:22). He asks God to grant the people the power to end famine through prayer: "If there is famine in the land then hear the prayer or supplication of every man among thy people Israel hear it in heaven thy dwelling and forgive, and act" (I Kings 8:37-39).

Solomon speaks of famine as a punishment given by God when the people have sinned: "when the heavens are shut up and there is no rain because thy servant and thy people Israel have sinned against thee ..." Solomon asks God to end famine at the point when the people realize their mistakes and ask for forgiveness: "when they pray towards this place ... hear in heaven and forgive their sin ... and grant rain." Rain becomes the symbol of God's forgiveness. This follows the narrator of *Ruth's* association of famine with an ineffective governing body. In her scenario, famine is inflicted on the people because of the corruption rampant during the time of the judges.

The conditions of the fields were read as an indicator of God's pleasure or displeasure with the people. In times of abundance, God rewarded the people for their actions. Famine meant that something was being done incorrectly. In Solomon's speech, the connection between God and the natural world is made explicitly. If the people are living responsibly, then God blesses them with rain and harvest; if they sin, the ground does not yield. In this way, the people are engaged in a dialogue with the natural world. External conditions are read as a sign of the community's spiritual health. Unfavorable ones force a period of self-reflection and change: the people must question why God has withdrawn. In a cyclic pattern, this questioning leads to reformation; reformation brings the forgiveness of God; and this forgiveness brings favorable conditions.

The best tenet of Solomon's version of the commandments is to allow strangers into the temple:

> The foreigner too, the man who does not belong to thy people Israel, but has come from a distant land because of thy fame, when he comes and prays towards this house, hear in heaven thy dwelling and respond to the call which the foreigner makes to thee, so that like thy people Israel all peoples of the earth may know thy fame and fear thee, and learn that this house which I have built bears thy name (8:41-43).

The King's desire for inclusivity in the state is modeled after his own home. Solomon has wives and courtiers from lands near and far. These women tell Solomon of their gods and Solomon speaks the name of his one God. As King of Jerusalem, he likes to show off his temple and spread his fame. By acting hospitably, Solomon earns a good name for himself and achieves peace.

In both I Kings and the book of Ruth, intermarriage is accepted and praised. Men and women from different places are bound to be intrigued by one another and such a union can be a good thing. As can the union by women from different cultures, like Ruth and Naomi. Solomon's first of many strategic marriages is to Pharaoh's daughter.

> Solomon allied himself to Pharaoh king of Egypt by marrying his daughter. He brought her to the City of David, until he had finished building his own house and the house of the Lord and the wall round Jerusalem (3:1-3).

The narrators of I Kings voice no objection to this marriage or to the fact that a special quarter is built for the Egyptian princess in Jerusalem. Solomon's marriage is hailed as being politically advantageous. The King does not stop with Pharaoh's daughter, but learns the customs of the entire region by having affairs with many women.

> King Solomon was a lover of women, and besides Pharaoh's daughter he married many foreign women, Moabite, Ammonite, Edomite, Sidonian, and Hittite, from the nations with whom the Lord had forbidden the Israelites to intermarry, "because," he said, "they will entice you to serve their gods." But Solomon was devoted to them and loved them dearly. He had seven hundred wives, who were princesses, and three hundred concubines (11:1-3).

At this point, the narrator voices an objection to Solomon's passion for foreign women. Emphasis is placed on the fact that Solomon consorts with women from "forbidden" nations. True to the consequence predicted in the prohibition against such marriages, Solomon becomes involved in worshiping other gods and goddesses. His wives show him their customs and Solomon proves an enthusiastic participant in their rituals.

> He followed Ashtoreth, goddess of the Sidonians and Milcom, the loathsome god of the Ammonites ... He built a hill-shrine for Kemosh, the loathsome god of Moab, on the height to the east of Jerusalem, and for Molech, the loathsome god of the Ammonites. Thus he did for the gods to which all his foreign wives burnt offerings and made sacrifices (11:5-8).

Solomon is chastised by the narrator and by God. The downfall of the monarchy is attributed to Solomon's departure from monotheism.

Despite the sharp criticism, Solomon's participation in these rituals gave him a broader sense of spiritual practice. Whether or not such activity distracted him from his relationship to the Israelite God, his participation in his wives' practices gave him knowledge of female worship. His wives may have schooled him in the feminine aspects of God and introduced him to a rich tradition of which he was not familiar. While such behavior is not deemed acceptable, Solomon's engagement in Goddess worship shows a deep respect for his wives' beliefs. Goddess worship is apparent in the structure of the temple itself. "The very manner in which Solomon's Temple was built in Jerusalem was conducive to the establishment of a polytheistic-syncretistic cult."[14] The innovations made by Solomon as he redesigned Israelite belief are a result of experimentation with other belief systems and the acceptance of neighboring cultures.

The book of Ruth traces King David's origin to a marriage between an Israelite man and a Moabite woman. As a canonized document, it lends support for Solomon's marriages and relationships. After all, Solomon could claim, a Moabite was his ancestress. It makes sense that a story supporting intermarriage would be written down and canonized during Solomon's time. Solomon could point to the pastoral tale as a precedent for cross-cultural marriage. After all, such a marriage was at the root of the monarchy.

The most intriguing tale of a visit paid to King Solomon is the story of the Queen of Sheba. The Queen hears of Solomon's legendary wisdom and travels on a caravan heavy with gifts so that she can appear before the king and test him with her riddles.

> The Queen of Sheba heard of Solomon's fame and came to test him with hard questions. She arrived in Jerusalem with a very large retinue, camels laden with spices, gold in great quantity, and precious stones. When she came to Solomon, she told him everything she had in her mind, and Solomon answered all her questions; not one of them was to abstruse for the king to answer. When the Queen of Sheba saw all the wisdom of Solomon, the house which he had built ... there was no more spirit left in her. Then she said to the king, 'The report which I heard in my own country about you and your wisdom was true, but I did not believe it until I came and saw for myself. Indeed I was not told half of it; your wisdom and your prosperity go far beyond the

report which I had of them ... Then she gave the king a hundred and twenty talents of gold, spices in great abundance, and precious stones. Never again came such a quantity of spices as the Queen of Sheba gave to King Solomon ... And King Solomon gave the Queen of Sheba all she desired, whatever she asked, in addition to all that he gave her of his royal bounty. So she departed and returned with her retinue to her own land (10:1-13).

According to James Pritchard, "the account of Sheba's visit bears the stamp of having been based on a formal, contemporary record of a memorable court occasion."[15] Yet, there are aspects of the story which suggest that the visit was more intimate than a formal, court occasion. The narrator does not specify the location. There is speculation that the land of Sheba was on the southern part of the Arabian peninsula and that the Shebans were the descendants of Abraham and his wife Keturah. Alternate Queen of Sheba myths claim that she is from Yemen or Ethiopia.

Beside where she comes from, the Queen evokes other mysteries. What where the riddles she asked Solomon? Why was Solomon's fame so compelling? To these questions, the Midrash has ready answers. The Midrash Mishle posits that the Queen's questions were a series of identity tests. Each riddle probes Solomon's knowledge of female matters or his ability to make gender distinctions. Her first riddle is:

What are they?
Seven depart and nine enter
two give drink but only one partakes.

Solomon answers:

No doubt, seven are the days of the menstrual cycle, nine are the months of pregnancy, two refers to the breasts and one to the child born who drinks from them.[16]

The Queen then offers another type of challenge. She presents Solomon with very young children of equal height, all dressed alike. "Distinguish the males from the females," she dares him. Solomon signals to his attendants and they bring him nuts and roasted grains which he spreads before the children. The males who are not embarrassed, gather them and place them in their garments. The females who are modest, place them in their headdresses. "Those are the males, and those are the females," Solomon says.

The midrash continues citing plausible riddles, each one testing Solomon's ability to make distinctions or his knowledge of natural order. Since the midrashic writers interpret a woman challenging Solomon as itself a test of natural order, it follows that they would assume her riddles to be an extension of her visit, the largest test.

The Queen does not come to blindly pay homage to the king. She comes to test Solomon in her own terms and determine if he deserves his reputation. The riddles could be anything from direct challenges of Solomon's power to an intricate mode of seduction. After testing him, the Queen is pleased with her results. She informs Solomon that the report she heard was true, but that she had to undertake the journey and see for herself. A match for Solomon, the Queen of Sheba dazzles him with her gifts and her knowledge. The narrator makes sure to say that the gift of spices exceeded any ever given to the king.

The relationship between the Queen of Sheba and Solomon, the great lover of women is left to our imagination. Intimacy is implied as the Queen tells Solomon "everything in her heart" (ot) and he responds by giving her "all that she desired." From all the accounts of Solomon's diplomatic relations, Sheba receives the most detailed description. Out of his one thousand lovers, the Queen is the only one with a complete story. A tremendous mystique surrounds this powerful woman who challenges Solomon and departs as easily as she appeared. The Queen's visit to Solomon is a meeting of Equals. The respect paid to The Queen of Sheba's story shows the gender equality of Solomon's time.

The Queen's story shares many similarities with the book of Ruth. Both women come from foreign lands and make a journey to Israel motivated by their desires and curiosities. The Queen of Sheba and Ruth take the initiative to approach powerful men. In the Queen's case, she challenges the King of Jerusalem and in Ruth's, she seeks out a wealthy landowner on the threshing floor. Neither the Queen nor Ruth are physically described. It as if their physical appearance becomes unimportant in light of their strength. The Queen of Sheba seeks Solomon's wisdom while Ruth seeks stability in Boaz's link to the land. Where the Queen's quest is completed in a short amount of time, Ruth remains in Bethlehem.

It is possible that the same scribe wrote the Queen's story and the book of Ruth. She may have been present when the Queen stayed at the court and read a subtext in the formal conversations of Solomon and the Queen. The same sensual mystery occurs in the description of Queen's visit and Ruth's night with Boaz on the threshing floor. The thematic and stylistic similarities between the story of the Queen of Sheba and the story of Ruth lead us to believe that the same woman wrote both of them. This scribe may have been the first female scribe allowed to write history and was able to record women's tales with a unique blend of sexual politics and female autonomy.

Notes

Chapter three: A Canonized Tale

1. *Ruth Rabbah,* Proem 2.

2. Bledstein, A.J. "Female Companionships: If the Book of Ruth Were Written by a Woman ..." in *A Feminist Companion to Ruth.* Brenner, A. ed. Sheffield Academic Press (England, 1993) 116-133.

3. Vallas, B.M. "The Book of Ruth and Its Purpose." *Theologia 25* (1954): 201-210.

4. Zenger, Erich. "Das Buch Ruth." in *Zuercher Bibelkommentare,* ed. by Henrich Schmid and Siegfried Schulz. (Zurich, Switzerland: Theologischer Verlag 1991).

5. Josephus. *Complete Works.*[20] William Whiston, tr. Kregel Publications (Grand Rapids, MI, 1985) 5:9, 4.

6. Hubbard, R.L. *The Book of Ruth.* Eerdman's Publishing (Grand Rapids, MI, 1988) 24.

7. Hubbard, R.L. Op. Cit., 50.

8. *Ruth Rabbah,* Proem 2.

9. May, H.G. *Oxford Bible Atlas.* Oxford University Press (New York, NY, 1984), 64.

10. For more information on post-menstrual purification laws, see Lev. 18:19; BMak, 14a; BNid 13b; 31b; 64b; BSanh. 37a; Gen. Rab. 17:13; Shulhan 'Arukh, Yareh De'ah 183.

11. Shakespeare, W. *Hamlet.* Willard Farnham, ed. Penguin Books (1985) II, ii.

12. May, H.G. Op. Cit., 64.

13. Goitein, S.D. "Megilat Ruth" in *Omanut ha-Sippur ba-Mikra 2,* (Jerusalem 1957) 2, 58-65.

14. Patai, R. Op. Cit., 39.

15. Pritchard, James. *Solomon and Sheba.* Phaidon (London, 1974), 10.

16. *Midrash Mishle*

CHAPTER FOUR:

FORTUNE'S REVERSAL

Biblical characters are as irrational, lustful, and ambitious as we are.
-Shira Sergant

FORTUNE'S REVERSAL

In the book of Ruth, the patriarchal order established in the majority of the Hebrew Bible is reversed. Women are the heroes while male characters occupy a position of secondary importance. Traditional roles are overturned in the narrative switch. With male concerns left in the background, female traditions only suggested in previous narratives are fleshed out. Ilana Pardes speaks of the book of Ruth's revisionist character, "as the marginal becomes central, the limitations of feminine perspectives elsewhere in biblical narrative are flaunted and challenged."[1] By altering the positions of male and female characters, the narrator makes a radical change in the nature of biblical journey stories while staying true to their form.

In the first ten lines, the narrator names three men from Bethlehem, tells who they married, then announces their deaths. Events are paired down to the bare essentials. The importance of Elimelech, Mahlon, and Chilion rests entirely in relation to the women characters. Their story is told quickly as a brief prelude to the real saga. The only other male scene, Boaz at the city gates, reads like a parody of patriarchal transactions. In contrast to Ruth and Naomi's swift execution of their plan to get a redeemer, the bombastic formality of the later male scene seems especially humorous.

While the implications of such a reversal are great, the narrator makes the switch so effectively that it causes no shock to the reader. Because the form is familiar, the innovation of placing women in central roles can be easily accepted. Perhaps the most stunning aspect of the book of Ruth is the manner in which the narrator employs and blends the conventions of male and female journey stories. Ruth's story is reminiscent of both Abraham and Sarah, Rachel and Jacob.

In *Ruth's* narrative structure, the two cycles meet.

Two aspects of *Ruth's* cyclic geometry stand out as innovations. First, the connection between the characters' experience and the harvest cycle is made explicitly. When famine is announced in the first line, we know that the characters will meet with a comparable emptiness in their own lives. When Ruth and Naomi arrive in Bethlehem "at the beginning of the barley harvest," we know that their unstable situation is on the way to improvement. The characters' journey corresponds with the harvest cycle.

Beyond making the famine/harvest parallel, the narrator of *Ruth* unifies another pair of opposites. She merges the male and the female journey sequences in the story of one family. While the Genesis narratives also chart the progress of one family, the male and the female stories follow separate cycles which intersect around the issue of childbirth. The two traditions are parallel, yet distinct. In the book of Ruth, a male experience precedes a female one. The movements of the men create a situation which requires a counter female movement. Two symmetrical journeys comprise the book's cycle.

ELIMELECH'S DESCENT

The narrative cycle begins with absence: "And it was in the days of the judges judging And there was famine in the land." Beginning with the same word, *va-Yehee*, these two statements create the setting. The repetition of *va-Yehee* (and it was) implies that these two situations not only coexist, but are also contingent upon each other. The rhythmic announcement of bad fortune is a rhetorical trick used by the narrator to suggest why the famine occurred. Repetition enforces the dual negativity of the situation: no effective leader and an insubstantial harvest.

The story opens in a down time characterized by what it lacks. Leadership has failed and the people lack sustenance. In a predominately agrarian society, the people may be indifferent to matters of politics, but famine is a materialization of deepest fear. Famine forces a recognition of humanity's dependency on the land as well as the limitations of such resources. Throughout biblical narratives, famine catalyzes change: a journey to an unknown place, a process of self-reflection, a shift in the dialogue with God. Because the earth does not yield, life cannot go on as it has before.

The Israelites perceived the presence of God in all steps of planting and harvesting. The season of planting was the time in which people would establish a relationship with God, and harvest meant the union's fruition. People labored in the fields, but in the end, it was something divine which allowed the crops to grow. Famine communicated that God had withdrawn. This absence was felt in the barren fields and hungry community. Famine caused farming practices as well as the spiritual health of the community to be called into question. Keeping in mind that the earth is the medium through which humanity and God communicate, a famine is a sign of a deficiency in the relationship. As stated by Joseph Campbell, "an abundant harvest is the sign of God's grace; God's grace is the food of the soul."[2] The reverse also holds true, the absence of God becomes evident in the absence of crops.

The midrash of Ruth Rabbah cites ten famines which have come upon the world:

> One in the days of Adam, one in the days of Lamech, one in the days of Abraham, one in the days of Isaac, one in the days of Jacob, one in the days of Elijah, one in the days of Elisha, one in the days of David, one in the days when the judges judged, and one which is destined to come upon the world.[3]

The recurrence of famine suggests that times of hardship will occur, pass and occur again. A problem in the relationship to God is always reparable through periods of reflection. That the tenth famine is still to come ties the contemporary world into the cycle of famine and plenty.

Along with the occurrence of famine, journeys catalyzed by famine are prevalent in biblical narrative. When there is no food, the protagonist will often leave home and seek a new situation. While such action is understandable, biblical narrators tend to condemn it. Each time a protagonist flees the land in search of better opportunity, he meets with disaster.

In Abraham's time, "there came a famine in the land, so severe that Abram went down to Egypt to live there for a while." Knowing that the Egyptians would not hesitate to murder him to acquire his beautiful wife, Abraham asks Sarah to pose as his sister. Sarah's agreement to the journey as well as to the facade is apparent in her actions.

> When Abram arrived in Egypt, the Egyptians saw that she (Sarah) was indeed very beautiful. Pharaoh's courtiers saw her and praised her to Pharaoh, and she was taken into Pharaoh's household. He treated Abram well because of her, and Abram came to possess sheep and cattle and asses, male and female slaves, she-asses and camels. But the Lord struck Pharaoh and his household with grave diseases on account of Abram's wife Sarai. Pharaoh summoned Abram and said to him, "Why have you treated me like this? Why did you not tell me that she is your wife? Why did you say that she was your sister, so that I took her as a wife? Here she is: take her and be gone." Then Pharaoh gave his men orders, and they sent Abram away with his wife and all that he had (Gen. 12:10-20).

In search of better fortune, Abraham misrepresents himself. Fearful of the Egyptians, he alters his identity in order to adapt to their society. Pharaoh chastises Abraham for his deception and for using his wife as a commodity of exchange. By departing from the land which God promised him, Abraham compromises his relationship with Sarah and with God. His attempt to assimilate results in a fragmentation of the family. Abraham witnesses his wife being taken into another man's house. No matter how temporary, such a split is contrary to God's vision of the "founding family."

After departing from Egypt, the family structure is further fragmented. Abraham and Lot part ways due to irreconcilable tensions between their herdsmen. As Abraham continues his journey, God instructs him to wander "the length and breadth of the land, for I give it to you" (13:17). God assigns Abraham to a specific region and asks him to remain there in times of plenty and disaster. Through the commitment to place, the relationship to God is solidified.

An almost identical story appears in the Isaac narrative. "There came (va-Yehee) a famine in land—not the earlier famine in Abraham's time—and Isaac went to Abimelech the Philistine king at Gerar" (Gen. 26:1). Before Isaac goes any farther, God appears and says to him: "Do not go down to Egypt, but stay in this country as I bid you. Stay in this country and I will be with you and bless you, for to you and to your descendants I will give all these lands" (Gen. 26:2-3). By intervening, God prevents Isaac from making Abraham's mistake. He informs Isaac that the blessing has boundaries. If Isaac travels outside of its parameters, he will be exposed to the world without God's protection.

At Abimelech's court, Isaac also creates the illusion that Rebekah is his sister. Abimelech takes Rebekah into the palace as his wife, only to discover that she is married to Isaac. This event coupled with Isaac's success in Gerar causes Abimelech to drive Isaac away. Even within the boundaries specified by God, Isaac has difficulties. To ensure his safety and independence, Isaac departs from the established Canaanite community and settles on the margins.

In the book of Ruth's opening, a man responds to the famine by fleeing his community. "There was a famine in the land and a man (from Bethlehem in Judah) went to live in the Moabite country with his wife and his two sons." We are introduced to the "man of Bethlehem in Judah" in the midst of his departure away from the very place which defines him. This type of emigration represents a descent, or a falling away from God's blessing. This man departs from Bethlehem (house of bread) and crosses the Jordan River to search for greener pastures. Instead of reflecting on the reason for the famine and how to change the situation, the man flees. He makes a definitive break from the covenantal land and settles on the river's opposite bank.

The weakness behind this type of retreat is indicated by its direct association with governmental chaos and famine. As the famine is linked to the judges judging, this man's flight in times of hardship indicates his tenuous belief in God's ability to change the situation. In the tripartite rhythm of the first line, the lack of order causes a lack of food which causes the man's lack of faith. As God has withdrawn from the fields, this man abandons his community. The midrash chastises him more directly:

> He was one of the notables of his place and one of the leaders of his generation. But when the famine came he said, "Now all Israel will come knocking at my door (for help,) each one of them with his basket." He therefore arose and fled from them.[4]

Elimelech initiates the departure. He is the only one associated with the action of leaving: "and a man went to live in the fields of Moab." His wife and two sons are mentioned afterward as if they followed without being consulted. The midrash says, "he was the prime mover, and his wife secondary to him, and his two sons secondary to both of them." They go to the fields of Moab, but are not condemned by the narrator. In the fields of Moab, the family from Bethlehem confront what is foreign as well as their own foreignness. They cannot be fulfilled in these fields because they lack connection to the soil. Such rootlessness is portrayed as yet another kind of emptiness.

The first line establishes set and setting in a skeletal form. The second line answers the vagueness by naming and locating the characters. The two lines balance each other by creating first a symbolic order and then a definitive one. The declaration of events followed by a more specific description is reminiscent of the call and response of an oral story. In an essay entitled *Ruth and Women's Culture*, Fokkelien van Dijk-Hemmes, working from Joseph Campbell's assertion that the audience participated in crafting parts of the story, writes "that oral transmission always happens in an interplay between narrator and public."[5] If we speak of *Ruth* in terms of an oral story, then the first line creates suspense that would be questioned by the audience and is filled in by the assignment of name and place.

The introduction of biblical characters follows different variations. Sometimes the main character is named and sometimes the character is described: "And Deborah a Prophetess, the wife of Lapidoth" (Jud. 4:4); "And there was a certain man of Zorah of the family of the Danites whose name was Manoah" (Jud. 13:2); "And there was a man of Mount Ephraim whose name was Micah" (Jud. 17:1); "And there was a man of Benjamin whose name was Kish" (I Sam. 9:1). In the book of Ruth, the sequence is as follows: "The man's name was Elimelech, his wife's name was Naomi, and the names of his two sons Mahlon and Chilion. They were Ephratites from Bethlehem in Judah." The mention of tribe and location gave the audience of the story clues about the person's character. The fact that the family members are "Ephratites from Bethlehem in Judah" would evoke a particular image in the minds of original audiences. A modern parallel would be a storyteller speaking of "a guy from Chicago" or "a real New Yorker." In both cases, the qualities of the character are contained in the description of origin.

In *Ruth*, the assertion of family and community helps to define the characters (Ruth is a virtuous Moabite, Boaz is Bethlehem's leading man of substance). All we are ever to know about Elimelech and his two sons is where they came from and where they went. By running away from the larger social structure of Bethlehem (the place which defined them), they negate their identity. According to Campbell, "from the standpoint or the way of duty, anyone in exile from the community is nothing."[6] Apart from the larger social structure, Elimelech and his sons are exiles, fragmented from a larger whole.

ELIMELECH, NAOMI'S HUSBAND

Knowing the sequence of famine, flight, and disaster from the stories of Abraham and Isaac, the consequence of Elimelech's emigration is jarring only in its severity. "Elimelech, Naomi's husband died, so that she was left with her two sons." Elimelech's end comes quickly before we have learned anything about his life in Moab. All we know of Elimelech is where he came from, who he married, and that he died. This brief report is reminiscent of those often used to describe biblical women who are named, get married, have children, and die. By using this technique to tell a man's story, the narrator redefines gender perspective.

Elimelech is referred to as "Naomi's husband" to signal that his importance in the story lies in the fact that he has changed the course of her life. He is relevant in terms of the woman who survives him. As readers, we do not become attached to Elimelech and care little about his fate. From the announcement of his death, our sympathies go to Naomi, the woman who remains in a foreign land. Naomi must face the future alone and redeem the actions of her husband.

We are given two textual clues as to why disaster strikes the Ephratite family. So that readers do not believe that death is random, the narrator encodes indicators of how the death fits into God's plan. Elimelech has left his home in times of hardship and "descended" to a foreign land. The syntax describing Elimelech's resettlement provides a clue for his abrupt end. The place where Elimelech resettles translates as the "fields of Moab." Elimelech does not bring his family to a town or to a community, but to "fields." Furthermore, the family does not reside in a specific field, but in the general "fields." This creates the sense that the family is living like a flock of sheep grazing in multiple pastures. In contrast to the lucid description of the family's origin, the place to which they emigrate is shrouded in ambiguity.

"The fields of Moab" is a symbolic description of space corresponding with "the days when judges judged," the unspecific description of time. The vagueness of time and space suggest the instability of the entire situation. The "fields of Moab" are the end point of this man's flight from God and community. These fields lack the blessing; the nourishment is so incomplete that all the men in the family meet their deaths. A no-man's land between Canaan and Moab, the fields are a place of shadow. The vagueness of time and space suggest the instability of the opening situation. Elimelech's actions are neutralized in the fields and then he dies. On the narrative level, the fields represent an empty, non-space corresponding with Sheol, the Hebraic notion of Hell.

Sheol appears in biblical narrative as an underworld, home to disembodied souls. "O Lord, thou hast brought me up from Sheol and saved my life as I was sinking into the abyss" (Ps. 30:3). The psalmist views Sheol as a void corresponding with the abyss of death. The verb 'ALH, *bring up*, lends to the sense of misery's depth. When Jacob laments Joseph's disappearance, he says: "I will go to my grave (Sheol) mourning for my son." (Gen. 37:35). The verb YRD, go down, locates Sheol beneath the earth. In Jacob's lament, Sheol is a physical place where he expects to find bottomless sorrow. In Greek, Sheol is translated as Hades (Job 26:6). Literally, Hades means grave or death, but is reified in mythology as the god of the nether world. Like Jacob (i.e. Israel), Hades shares a name with his land.

The myth of Hades, Persephone, and Demeter shares many themes with the book of Ruth. Demeter, the goddess of the cornfield, was famous for her gentle soul until her daughter, Persephone, was abducted by Hades. Hades, in love with Demeter at first sight, asked Zeus' permission to marry her. Zeus did not want to offend his eldest brother, yet feared Demeter's wrath. Zeus responded to the request by saying that he would neither forbid nor consent to the marriage. While picking poppies in a field, Persephone was kidnapped by Hades. In search of her daughter, Demeter wandered the earth and, in her sorrow, prevented any crops from growing. Zeus sent a message to Hades that unless he returned Persephone, all life would end and a message to Demeter that Persephone would be returned on the condition that she had not eaten the food of the dead. Because Persephone had eaten seven pomegranate seeds, a compromise was made that Persephone would spend three months of the year with Hades and the other nine with Demeter.

The other noun used for Sheol is *Tanaton* as we find it in II Samuel 22:6. These two nouns refer to the world below, a place of darkness and death. While *Hades* emphasizes the place of death and the world below, *Tanatos* refers to the shadow of death. Due to the perception of the LXX, we suggest that the death of Elimelech cannot be perceived as a natural one.

The manner in which Elimelech settles in the fields of Moab reinforces his marginality. "And they came to the fields of Moab and were there." (ot) The narrator uses the verb HYH (to be), not HYH (to live) to convey the ephemerality of the settlement. Residing in the fields, the family remains unabsorbed in Moabite culture. The midrash interprets the settlement in the fields as part of a larger wandering. "At first they came to the cities, but they found the inhabitants steeped in transgression. They then went to the large cities and found a dearth of water. They thereupon returned to the cities, and they came to the fields of Moab and continued there."[7] In this description, Elimelech's options are limited by cultural differences as well as by a lack of natural resources. The fields are selected by default. Unable to find the ideal place to live, Elimelech and his family choose the lesser of all evils.

After Elimelech dies, Naomi and her sons do not leave the fields of Moab. Mahlon and Chilion further assimilate to the culture on the other side of the river as they take their first independent action. "These sons married Moabite women, one of whom was called Orpah and the other Ruth, and they had lived there about ten years, when both Mahlon and Chilion died, so that the woman was bereaved of her two sons as well as of her husband" (Ruth 1:4-5). Mahlon and Chilion attempt to blend with Moabite culture by marrying Moabite women. That Mahlon's and Chilion's life in Moab is more permanent than their father's is evidenced by the verb *va-Yeshvu* (they dwelled). In contrast to Elimelech's settlement (and they were there), Mahlon and Chilion establish themselves in the fields. Perhaps such adaptation represents transgression, or perhaps, Mahlon and Chilion are punished for their father's flight. As God stated to Moses, "I punish the children for the sins of the fathers." Whatever the cause, the two sons also perish in the fields.

In her essay about the book of Ruth, Mieke Bal states, "more often than not, biblical names have a meaning, if they do not have one, they are assigned one in the text's afterlife."[8] Disaster is imminent in the names of the two sons. The midrash explains, "Mahlon, in that they were blotted out (nimhu) from the world, and Chilion, in that they perished (kalu) from the world."[9] One wonders if the storyteller uses the characters of the sons as prototypes of incompetent men. The fact that they are in Moab for "about ten years" is also meaningful. Ten years is the period during which couples are expected to have children: "If a man married a woman and remained with her for ten years and had no children, he is not permitted to refrain from procreation."[10] Mahlon and Chilion produce no offspring with their

Moabite brides. Perhaps they were unable to continue the family line because they had been subsumed in the negative space of the fields of Moab. They could no more reproduce than the fields could sustain the family. In this transitional region, Mahlon and Chilion are paralyzed before they meet their death.

NAOMI'S RESURRECTION

After the deaths of Elimelech, Mahlon, and Chilion, the focus turns to Naomi. As readers, we look to Naomi for an explanation of the disaster and expect to hear one in her mourning. Instead, we witness Naomi taking swift action to separate herself from tragedy and return home.

> Then she arose with her daughters-in-law, that she might return from the fields of Moab for she had heard in the field of Moab that the Lord had visited his people in giving them bread. So she went to the place where she was, and her two daughters-in-law with her; and they took the road to return to the land of Judah (Ruth 1:6-8).

Naomi's first action is rising. She emerges from the ashes of disaster like a phoenix reborn and distances herself from death. Naomi rises as the family head and claims her independence. Although disaster causes the reclamation of power, Naomi handles herself calmly and acts with strength. The action of rising (*vatakom*) signals Naomi's rebirth and the beginning of her personal journey. As well as rising out of exile's darkness, Naomi steps up as a heroine. She rises from the obscurity designated for female characters and commands the story.

Naomi's forward motion is described in a three-verb sequence: *va-Takom, va-Tashav, va-Teşeh*. Three is a recurring number in the book of Ruth representing stability. Corresponding with the triangular covenant (humanity-earth-God), the appearance of tripartite sequences suggests that the covenant is being honored. By embarking on the road home, Naomi moves closer to God's blessing. The notion that she never wanted to move to Moab is enforced by her immediate departure.

The reason given for Naomi's decision is that "she had heard in the field of Moab that the Lord had visited his people in giving them bread." In rumor, Naomi finds hope of deliverance. It is important to note that although Naomi makes the decision to leave the "fields of Moab" (plural), she receives her information in the "field of Moab" (singular). A change of location is already apparent. Use of the singular implies that there was a specific field designated for gathering and the transmission of news.

The field (singular) also calls to mind the image of Naomi at a marketplace receiving information about conditions in the land of Judah. This image is reinforced by midrashic commentary: "she heard from peddlers making their rounds from city to city."[11] In this interpretation, traveling merchants brief Naomi on Bethlehem's improved conditions and she acts on this advice.

Since fields are the biblical landscape where supernatural encounters occur, a plausible interpretation is that Naomi hears of God's return from an angel, or a messenger of God. According to the Aramaic storyteller:

> And she returned from the field because she was informed in the field of Moab by the words of an angel that God remembered his people, the house of Israel to give them bread on the account of the merit of Ibzan the leader and his prayer ... he is Boaz the pious.[12]

In the Aramaic story, Naomi is driven to return home after receiving supernatural guidance. This angelic encounter is similar to that of Samson's mother who met, in the field, a man whose "countenance was like the countenance of an angel of God" (Jud. 13:6).

Another possibility is that Naomi "hears" this information intuitively because she longs for her native place. In such a scenario, it is an inner voice which propels her. What Naomi hears is powerful enough to set her in motion. The fragment of a story within a story indicates the importance of oral transmission. Once she hears of God's return, the preparation for a new life begins. News restores Naomi's faith in an information transfer which eludes to a developed system of transcultural communication.

Departing from the fields of Moab, Naomi, Ruth, and Orpah separate themselves from disaster. The recognition of harvest in Bethlehem foreshadows their return to a healthy situation. As well as being a feminist journey story, the book of Ruth is a story of survival. Each narrative landscape represents a step in the movement from death to life. On this level, the story is a parable of overcoming hardship. The first restorative motion is the road to return.

THE ROAD TO RETURN

Naomi and her Moabite daughters-in-law begin the walk together. "So she went out of the place where she was, and her two daughters-in-law with her; and they took the road to return to the land of Judah" (Ruth 1:7). The path twists out of the fields of Moab and leads in the direction of Judah, Naomi's home territory. The road to return is a liminal landscape on the border between Israel and Moab, a place where the three women are not subject to patriarchal laws. Naomi and her daughters-in-law can set their own rules and conduct their own rituals of mourning. In this state of flux, the three women have total freedom. The road to return is the place of their liberation.

Naomi, Ruth, and Orpah embark on the road together, unified in the desire to leave tragedy behind them. For the first time, the women's voices are heard. Ironically, the widows do not engage in mourning, but in a discussion of the future. Naomi, Ruth, and Orpah speak to each other about each other. The intimacy these women have developed becomes apparent in the dialogue's tenderness.

Naomi addresses Ruth and Orpah with a blessing:

> Then Naomi said to her two daughters-in-law, "Go back, both of you, to your mother's homes. May the Lord keep faith with you, as you have kept faith with the dead and with me; and may he grant each of you security in the home of a new husband" (Ruth 1:8-9).

On the way back to her place of origin, Naomi advises Ruth and Orpah to do the same. She emphasizes the importance of female support during times of sorrow by telling her daughters-in-law to return to their mother's homes. Traditionally, a widow or a woman who failed to perform the proper wifely duties was sent back to her father's house as a sign of disgrace. Naomi advises Ruth and Orpah to return home without the customary stigma, thus making reference to a matriarchal system. She does not send them back to their fathers to be treated as possessions, but to their mothers to seek solace and refuge.

Naomi begins to make the split from her daughters-in-law by expressing her gratitude and directing them home. She speaks to her Moabite daughters-in-law in terms of YHWH (the Hebrew God). Apparently, Ruth and Orpah are familiar with the Hebrew God, because Naomi blesses them in His name. She praises the actions of her daughters-in-law by wishing that God treat them in the same manner. Naomi releases Ruth and Orpah from obligations to the memory of her sons by telling them to seek "security in the home of a new husband." She does not want the young women to live as widows, but to remarry, have children, and begin a new life. Although Naomi urges Ruth and Orpah to forget their sorrow and continue their lives, a vague resentment permeates her blessing. After all, Naomi has no mother to return to and little hope of remarrying. She loves her daughters-in-law and desires their well-being, but the subtext indicates Naomi's personal fears.

To finalize the blessing, Naomi "kissed them; and they lifted up their voice, and wept." This is the first mention of grief on the part of the widows. The women are not seen crying after the deaths of their husbands, but when faced with separation from one another. The road to return is a place of female bonding where the women conduct a ritual of mourning and redefinition. The collective action after the blessing follows the three verb sequence, adding to the sense of ceremony and to the notion that female assembly is a form of upholding the covenant.

Ruth and Orpah respond to Naomi's call: "Then they said to her, 'We will return with you to your own people.'" They plan to continue the walk with Naomi into a foreign land. Not prepared to separate, Ruth and Orpah express a solidarity which transcends cultural barriers.

Naomi responds to their declaration by evaluating her own sense of worth.

> But Naomi said, "Go back, my daughters. Why should you go with me? Am I likely to bear any more sons to be husbands for you? Go back, my daughters, go. I am too old to marry again. But even if I could say that I had hope of a child, if I were to marry this night and if I were to bear sons, would you then wait until they grew up? Would you then refrain from marrying? No, no my daughters, my lot is more bitter than yours, because the Lord had been against me" (Ruth 1:11-14).

In the supplication, Naomi articulates her deepest grief and commands Ruth and Orpah to turn away from her. By telling them to "go back," Naomi wishes their return to a state of innocence and safety. She does not want the young women to be tainted by her pain. Naomi's self-depreciation is based on the fact that she cannot have children, in other words, on a patriarchal standard.

Because Naomi cannot bear children and does not expect to ever have an heir, redemption seems impossible. Naomi interprets her post-menopausal state as a barrier between her and God. Her doubt goes beyond that of Sarah who asked, "After I am waxed old shall I have pleasure ... Shall I of surety bear a child, when I am old?" (Gen. 18:12-13). By asserting that she is "too old to marry again," or "bear any more sons," Naomi shows that she has internalized the famine. An older woman neglecting her inner-vision, Naomi evaluates herself in external terms. I am not young, she tells her daughters comparing herself to them.

Ruth and Orpah again lift their voices and weep. "Then Orpah kissed her mother-in-law and returned to her people, but Ruth clung to her" (Ruth 1:14). Convinced by Naomi's words, Orpah makes no further protest. She kisses her mother-in-law and disappears. Ruth clings to Naomi. In the absence of men, the women realign themselves and define new relationships. Naomi acts as family head, but does not assume a patriarchal stance. She offers the freedom of decision to her daughters-in-law. The fact that Orpah and Ruth make different choices shows the veracity of Naomi's gift. Orpah splits from Naomi and Ruth joins with her.

As Orpah walks into the distance, Naomi urges Ruth to follow suit: "'You see,' said Naomi, 'Your sister-in-law has gone back to her people and to her gods; Go back with her'" (Ruth 1:15). Naomi expresses diminished confidence in herself and in her God. She implores Ruth to leave her side and escape Naomi's shadow. Not wanting to accept responsibility for Ruth's future, Naomi tries to push her away.

Ruth resists Naomi's attempts at devaluation and speaks to the woman that Naomi is, not the woman she appears to be. The patriarchal order is negated as Ruth makes an alliance based on a feminine value system. Ruth provides Naomi with a reason to live and assures her mother-in-law that the judgments of a male world have little relevance. She answers Naomi with a pledge of determination.

> "Do not urge me to go back and desert you," Ruth answered. "Where you go, I will go, and where you stay, I will stay. Your people shall be my people, And your God my God Where you die, I will die and there I will be buried. I swear a solemn oath before the Lord Your God: Nothing but death shall divide us" (1:16-18).

In the reflexivity of her words, Ruth dissolves the boundary between her and Naomi. Ruth places her mother-in-law above any love or deity, and erases her past with five verbs. Nothing more is mentioned of Ruth's history, other than the fact that she is a Moabite.

Ruth silences Naomi's protest by vowing to act as her extension and absorbs the older woman's bitterness into her youth. She counters self-depreciation with transcendent love. By halting Naomi's discourse, Ruth moves to the next stage of the journey: the matter of getting home. With reflexive verbs, Ruth pledges to transcend all cultural and ideological barriers. Reminiscent of a wedding vow, Ruth fuses her life with Naomi's. That Ruth does not name any particular road, destination, culture, or God shows that her decision is not self-serving.

Ruth calls on the God which Naomi feels has abandoned her as a witness. Having sensed Naomi's tenuous faith, Ruth refers to God's power of decision. She mentions God between two statements about death, reminding Naomi that God will determine her time of death. Ruth makes mention of death twice ("where you die, I will die"; "nothing but death shall divide us") as if to show Naomi that Ruth suspects her motivation in setting out alone. The bond which Ruth forges with Naomi can only be broken by death. Ruth tells Naomi that like Elimelech and his sons, they will die in the same place ("and there I will be buried"). Ruth plans no return to Moab. Her actions reflect another biblical recommendation to "choose life, that both thou and thy seed may live" (Deut. 30:19).

By speaking these words, Ruth performs her first life-giving act. She does not let Naomi wander into the wilderness alone, but commits herself to Naomi's survival. The strength of Ruth's words may come from the passion of having made a decision or because she wants to hear no further arguments. Ruth mentions no aspect of the past nor any previous alliance that she had with her husband, Mahlon. Ruth's pledge overturns all past loyalties to create an innovative partnership.

In contrast to the concise declaration of Elimelech's journey, Naomi's and Ruth's decision-making process is dynamic and emotional. No words are ever spoken by Elimelech, Mahlon, and Chilion, and Naomi does not raise her voice until after their deaths. The women are first heard in dialogue regarding the future. Where Elimelech's migration was a rapid descent into disaster, Naomi's rise is a process of healing. The back and forth exchanges, the climax of Ruth's passionate pledge, and the three stages of Naomi's resolve lend a ritualistic cadence to the road to return.

Ruth and Naomi are the perfect team. Naomi has the strategy and Ruth has the strength. In their relationship, the opposites of youth and age, wisdom and beauty, native and stranger are unified. Difference disappears because Ruth and Naomi share the same goal. Their paths not only run parallel, but are fused. The balance achieved by their partnership ensures their success.

LIKE THELMA AND LOUISE

The female buddy story is alive and well in the 20th century. On the silver screen, the archetypes of women adventurers appear as Thelma and Louise, two disengaged American women. Thelma and Louise become fugitives who depart from a patriarchal world and define their own code of ethics. Their story begins as they pack up for a road trip, the great American adventure sure to be filled with gas stations, drinking, and rock-n-roll. Louise, the older and haunted protector, and Thelma, the innocent housewife, depart from repressive situations to find freedom in the desert.

The two women take to the highway decked out in lipstick and matching accessories, but not before Thelma leaves her husband dinner and Louise records a message for her neglectful, musician boyfriend. The first stop is a road side bar replete with the same dangers as the fields of Bethlehem. Like the fields, the bar is just off the road, set away from the community. It is a sexual environment where men preying on women is permissible and, perhaps, a microcosm of the larger society. Thelma encounters Harlan, the local slimeball, who gets her drunk, spins her on the dance floor, and leads her to the parking lot. Becoming increasingly menacing, Harlan holds Thelma down, assaults her, and prepares to rape her. Thelma's cries of "no!" do nothing to stop him. Louise appears on the scene and saves her friend by pulling out a gun and aiming it at Harlan. Burning with fury, Louise instructs him that "when a woman's crying like that, she's not having any fun." Harlan responds with "I should have fucked her," and "suck my cock." Louise shoots him dead.

Thelma and Louise, like Ruth and Naomi, find themselves faced with a man's death and drive away on an undefined road of return. Louise sets her sights on Mexico, a promised land where she can find protection from the wrath of the law. "I'm going to Mexico," she announces to Thelma and gives her a choice. Thelma takes time to think it over and makes two futile calls to her husband. Outside of a convenience store, she asks Louise, "how long till we're in God-damn Mexico?" Thelma solidifies her commitment to Louise as the soundtrack sings, "you're a part of me. I'm a part of you."

The rhythm intensifies as Thelma and Louise transform into outlaws who, in facing the wilderness, bear a remarkable resemblance to the matriarchs of *Genesis* who move away from establishment to found a new community. While following a tradition of pioneer women, Thelma and Louise speed into a predominately hostile world. They pass up the cowboy and the musician, two sympathetic yet incompetent men to continue on the road. The heroines' bold and decisive action is contrasted by the "male assembly" of police, CIA agents, and Thelma's husband who band together to track the women down. The men of the movie are more dangerous then the men at the gates of Bethlehem and offer threats in place of praise. Misunderstood by the power structure, Thelma and Louise pull out guns and get revenge on a phallo-centric system.

As they move farther away from society, Thelma and Louise become more rugged and natural. When they find success in gun-slinging, a CIA man confesses to a cop, "I can't tell if they're real smart or real lucky." Unlike Ruth and Naomi, Thelma's and Louise's redemption can only occur through a complete break from the male world. Nothing about the patriarchy offers them sanctuary. Because they cannot return to a community, they must create one of their own. As they go deeper in the desert, Thelma and Louise's love becomes more apparent. In the spirit of Ruth, Thelma tells Louise: "Something's crossed over in me, I can't go back, I mean, I just couldn't live." Thelma describes her transformation in terms of "something crossing over." Catalyzed by Harlan's death, the freedom she experiences makes her feel alive for the first time. Thelma's oath parallels Ruth's who swore to Naomi that "nothing but death shall divide us." Louise smiles at the pledge and answers, "don't wanta end up on the damn Hiraldo show." Thelma and Louise remain together until death. The final scene finds them surrounded by police cars and men with guns. They choose not to look back, but kiss each other and accelerate. Thelma and Louise drive into the Grand Canyon, the great American abyss.

Ruth combines wit and daring in order to make patriarchal laws of charity and marriage work for her. To survive, she must use the laws to her own benefit. Ruth's independence secures a place for her and Naomi in Bethlehem and her seduction reestablishes the family. Thelma and Louise have no such option. As Louise repeatedly reminds Thelma, the laws are not designed for their benefit. Because the law cast them into the roles of villains, they become outlaws. No matter how smart or lucky they may be, they cannot survive in the male world. Thelma and Louise choose death because any other option would require submission to a system they have vowed to confront. Where Ruth and Naomi demonstrate their heroism by reintegrating into society, Thelma and Louise pave a path away from the patriarchy and into the chasm.

THE SILENT JOURNEY

Once Naomi comprehended the extent of Ruth's determination, "she said no more, and the two of them went until they came to Bethlehem." Naomi's saying "no more" does not necessarily mean that the two women travel in silence, but that the nature of their conversation changes. Moving toward Bethlehem, Naomi and Ruth share moments hidden from the readers. We refer to this portion of the story as "the silent journey" because the narrator describes nothing of the trip between the fields of Moab and Bethlehem. We do not know by what means the two women traveled, whom they encountered, or what they discussed.

Typical of biblical travels, only the points of departure and arrival are named. A geographic analysis reveals that Ruth and Naomi would have to cross the Jordan River and the Judean Desert in order to reach Bethlehem. Since the journey between Moab and Bethlehem would take between four and five days, we can be sure that the terrain presented a challenge and that Naomi and Ruth shared extensive dialogue.

During this "silent journey," Naomi may describe life in Bethlehem: the important families, harvest rituals, and town customs. Ruth's later request to "go to the fields and glean ears of corn after him in whose sight I shall find favor" shows her knowledge of the Israelite system of charity. Naomi may conspire with Ruth to reclaim a piece of land which belonged to Elimelech. In this case, Ruth is well aware of Boaz's existence before she arrives in his fields. This background information is suggested by the narrator when Ruth, "as chance would have it," finds herself in Boaz's fields.

A woman in a man's world, Naomi must use subterfuge in requisitioning her land. The existence of this parcel of land is not overtly mentioned until Boaz negotiates his marriage with the elders outside of the city gates. Since Naomi does not have the ability to march into town and demand her land, she must manipulate events to her favor. As the pieces of the story come together, Naomi's plan to regain her land becomes apparent. Naomi is not only driven to return to the land of her birth, but to regain her land. The plan is executed by Ruth, who acts as Naomi's extension.

Ruth and Naomi do not lie fallow in the fields of Moab, but plant the seeds of their future. The emphasis in this undescribed dialogue is that Ruth and Naomi had their destination in sight and did not falter until they arrived. Unlike Elimelech, "and a man went," Ruth and Naomi provide each other with support, "the two of them went." Naomi has completed the cycle of her husband's journey and has returned home on her own terms.

The midrash of Ruth Rabbah imagines that the two women discussed Israelite practice and attended a festival. Their attendance at such an event is interpreted as a sin: "They transgressed the letter of the Law and journeyed on the Festival. The way was hard for them ... And they went discussing the laws of proselytes."[13] Since Ruth and Naomi arrive in Bethlehem at "the beginning of the barley harvest," it can be suggested that they began their journey on the

Passover festival. While movement during the Passover is defined as a transgression, Ruth and Naomi, like the children of Israel, travel in the name of freedom.

Another concealed element of the silent journey is the crossing of the Jordan River. Although the narrator makes no mention of this passage, the traversal from the fields of Moab to Bethlehem would entail such a crossing. The Bible Atlas locates "the plains of Moab" north of the Dead Sea in the Arabah Valley between the Jabbok River and Wadi Hesban. For Naomi and Ruth to reach the Land of Judah, they would have to forge the Jordan River.

Crossing the Jordan River is always documented as a momentous event. Whether for trade, war, or exploration, the passage across the water entails a transformation. The river is a natural boundary which divides a valley into two separate banks. It appears in narrative as a symbol of transition between home and exile, life and death, the familiar and the strange. The return to Judah requires the crossing of the Jordan. Crossing the Jordan is a process of purification and return. Naomi's crossing of the water would serve as a final cleansing of the disaster of Moab. The dust of foreign soil would be washed away in the water's currents. For Ruth, crossing the Jordan would be a step in her conversion to Israelite belief.

In three other biblical stories, crossing a body of water precedes dramatic change. When Moses is lifted from the Nile by Pharaoh's daughter, a leader/savior escapes death. When Moses leads the people across the Red Sea, he brings a nation of slaves from a landscape of forced toil into the desert where they test the parameters of freedom. Although the waters separate, crossing the Red Sea represents the first stage of transformation in the people of Israel's journey. Coming from a foreign land considered spiritually unclean, a national baptism is necessary to wash away the mark of exile.

Joshua, leader of Canaan's resettlement, leads the generation born wandering in the wilderness across the Jordan River and into the promised land. Like the Red Sea, the Jordan splits to allow for passage. Joshua is instructed by God to lay four stones on the bottom of the river-bed to symbolize the eternal cleansing of the people of Israel. With this crossing, the people of Israel put an end to a nomadic period.

And Joshua rose early in the morning; and they removed from Shittim, and came to the Jordan, he and all the children of Israel. And spent the night there before they passed over. And it came to pass after three days, that the officers went through the camp; and they commanded the people, saying, when you see the Ark of the Covenant of the Lord your God, and the priests the Levites bearing it, then you shall remove from your place, and go after it, that you may know the way by which you must go: for you have not passed this way heretofore ... And Joshua said to the people, "Sanctify yourselves: for tomorrow the Lord will do wonders among you" (Josh. 3:1-6).

Joshua imparts the significance of this crossing by reminding the people of the first passage. "For the Lord your God dried up the waters of the Jordan from before you, until you were passed over, as the Lord God did to the Red Sea" (4:23). The crossing of the Jordan takes place in the spring and represents a seasonal transformation as well as temporal change.

Both Joshua's and Naomi and Ruth's passages occur at the beginning of harvest. From the story of Joshua, we know that such a crossing is challenging, "for the Jordan overflows all its banks throughout the time of harvest." Since Ruth and Naomi arrive in Bethlehem at the beginning of the barley harvest, we can assume that the Jordan "overflows all its banks" as in Joshua's time. Ruth's and Naomi's steps toward return follow the course of the people of Israel returning to their land. Ruth and Naomi represent a nation of women emerging with new strength.

The silent journey is the second level of redemption. With the simultaneous mention and concealment of this journey, the narrator speaks to the nature of grief. After the emotional articulations made on the road to return, the heroines need a quiet, internal time. Traveling from Moab to Bethlehem represents a transitional period during which Ruth and Naomi sever themselves from the past and move toward a restorative future.

Crossing the Jordan is an integral part of the transformation. The water renews the women and cleanses them of their husbands' deaths. We can imagine a ceremony in which Naomi and Ruth bathe together and wash away some of their anguish. This crossing of water symbolizes Naomi's purification after living in a pagan land and Ruth's baptism into a new belief system. After forging the river, the women traverse the Judean desert on the way to Bethlehem. The arduous journey solidifies their friendship.

The last leg of Ruth and Naomi's exodus entails walking the road to Ephrath (Bethlehem), the place where Rachel died.

Rachel's death ... encapsulates her unfulfilled yearnings, her tragic exile. She dies on the way–not far from Ephrath, but not fully there. Bearing in mind that Ephrath is Bethlehem, the location of her tomb is not without significance. This liminal locus intonates that she makes it to the threshold of the royal city but is not allowed to enter. The future Davidic dynasty does not spring from her sons, but from Judah, Leah's fourth son.[14]

Like Rachel, Ruth has left the land of her birth in the name of love. Both women walk the road to Bethlehem as strangers. "The book of Ruth begins where the story of Rachel ends: on the way to Bethlehem, between two lands, in a double exile."[15] Ruth picks up Rachel's dreams and carries them into Bethlehem. As she finds a new love and begins the Davidic line, Ruth fulfills Rachel's quest.

THE SILENT JOURNEY:
A STORY OF THE PASSAGE OF NAOMI AND RUTH

The following fictional presentation is a midrash, a story based on a biblical tale.

Day 1: <u>Where You Go, I Will Go</u>

A life of tents was never expected of me. As I girl, I never learned this particular art. It was my husband Mahlon who taught me. Before his death, I often accompanied Mahlon and his flocks to the wilderness of Moab. If we got lost in the darkness, Mahlon would reassure me with laughter. He would say, "We are safe. I am a Hebrew destined for a life of wandering and tents." Strange that it was a Hebrew who taught me the terrain of my native land. He taught me what to eat in the wilderness, how to make alliances with things unseen, how to negotiate paths.

Yet on the path I traveled away from Moab, it was not Mahlon whom I walked with but his mother, Naomi. Both of our husbands were dead and Naomi was determined to return to her native town of Bethlehem. How could I let an old woman travel alone?

So I joined her in a return to a place I knew only through stories. Part of me expected Naomi to have this path mapped out in her memory and to navigate with the great Hebrew instinct. But I soon realized that Naomi was depending on me to lead her back to her home.

We didn't walk far that first day. We covered a few miles in silence and then stopped in the wilderness of Moab. It had been a long time since I had sent a tent. Naomi sat on a rock and watched me as I raised the sticks and cloth. Perhaps it had been a long time since she had seen a tent rising. Perhaps since her husband Elimelech had first brought her to Moab.

I never knew Elimelech or much about him. Mahlon had refused to talk about him. "What's there to know, he fled our home in Bethlehem during times of famine and brought us here." And if I asked Mahlon how Elimelech had died, he would say, "From the disease of here."

I had wanted to ask Naomi these questions that my husband would never answer. So while I set the tent, I did. But when I questioned the cause of Elimelech's death, Naomi turned her face from me and would not answer. From that moment on, I knew that we had an agreement to never speak the name of the dead. So "the disease of here" was all I was ever to know of Elimelech's end.

Wrapped in dusk, we sat outside the tent. I busied myself by counting stars and giving them funny names while Naomi rocked herself back and forth whispering, "your people are my people; your God my God; where you die, I will die; and there I will be buried." These words were mine. Yet each time I caught a piece of her whispering, it had a different meaning to me than when I had said the words myself. I thought, "perhaps Naomi will one day give these words to other women as a song, perhaps they will be passed down from generation to generation, perhaps my words will live forever." When we lay inside the tent, Naomi finally spoke words that were not my own. "I am returning like the wanton children of Israel after slavery. But you Ruth, you are a traveler as Abraham was a traveler." Then, I swear, I heard the old woman giggle. I thought to ask her why she giggled, but I understood her words to be a piece of a larger puzzle.

Day 2: <u>The Wind in the Palms</u>

When I woke, Naomi's eyes were lifted toward the sun. "Ruth, you must learn to rise early when the sun faces you like a lover. If you sleep too long, the sun will meet you face to face like an enemy." I turned my face toward hers and she turned hers toward mine. "Mother," I said, "I have heard that the water of the Salt Sea soothes the muscles. I would like to be soothed before we continue." "So we go," she said as she rose.

I had laid eyes on the Salt Sea only once before, but had floated there many times in dreams. As we walked toward the sea, I remembered a dream. *I was floating in the sea alone. The only sound was the sound of my legs splashing the water until a voice called out to me, "Ruth, are you listening?" "Who is there," I asked. "El Shaddai," was the voice's answer. When I looked around me, I saw no one there. I was still alone but I no longer felt alone.*

When the sun was highest and facing us like an enemy, we stopped for shade and drink by a spring. Cupping water in her palms, Naomi said, "I cannot cross the water tonight." "We are safe," I replied, "we will camp next to the water and cross tomorrow." I didn't know where I was going, but I hoped my reassurance would keep Mahlon's voice alive and comfort Naomi.

It grew dark as we moved toward the Salt Sea. Even in blackness, the air felt thick and hot. We were lucky that some light breezes cut through the heat and cooled us. I felt alliance with the wind, for it traveled as I was traveling. With this wind sweeping across the desert, I first understood what I was doing. I was leaving behind both of the lives that I had known earlier: the life of a daughter and the life of a wife.

True, I had married a foreign Hebrew. But to me, this was not unusual. I grew up listening to my father's tales of the wandering Hebrews. As a girl, I would wake at the sound of his sandals moving across the courtyard and run to him. He would lean down to stroke my head and look at me with eyes made wild by the fire.

"Have you come for your story, you little beggar," he would tease, then he would sit me on his knee and begin, "And it was in those days of long ago." He told many kinds of stories, but we both favored the tales of the Hebrews and their invisible God.

When the young Mahlon first came to tea at our house, my father clapped his hands and said, "I always knew it would be a Hebrew." So I left my father's house and went to Mahlon's. How different this departure from that one. That time, I was transferred from father's hands to Mahlon's and exchanged for some sheep. It was I who chose this path.

The wind in the palms brought me back to the night, to the half moon and the stars. Naomi and I walked until we came to a flat hilltop. "The night is so warm that we do not have to raise a tent," I told her. We lay down blankets and I thanked the winds before falling asleep.

Day 3: The Mikvah in the Jordan

Naomi sat at the edge of the hilltop holding her legs in her hands like a basket. I followed her line of vision to the sea which glowed before us in the morning sun. "Sweet waters of the Jordan, you travel to this place and become bitter and undrinkable. My life, my life was once so sweet," Naomi seemed to say to the sea. I rose from the blankets and held her in my arms. She rested her uncovered head on my shoulder. I saw the toll of the desert in her hair, the miles of dust, the tangles of sleeping in a tent and not using oils.

"Look at us," I said, "Let's get in that Salt Sea and have it make us beautiful."

"The sea is not as you expect."

I smiled. "I like surprises."

We gathered our things and went down to the shore. I stood startled when Naomi began to take off all of her clothes. "Ruth, it is allowed. Women often come to bathe in the Salt Sea." I made no move to undress until she assured me several times that this was permissible. I started laughing when I took off all my clothes and didn't stop until Naomi and I were immersed in the water and realized that we couldn't sink. We floated on our backs and raised our legs high in the air. We bobbed up and down, waved our hands wildly, and kept laughing. I paddled away from Naomi and looked to the sky. "El Shaddai, are you with me," I asked. And I knew that the answer was "Yes."

When we got out of the water, the sun was already high and our bodies were covered in the oils of the sea. "Naomi, I don't want to put on my skirt and robes, my body's so oily." "Don't worry, when we cross the Jordan the oils will wash away," she said. I understood then that after crossing the river, we would be in the legendary land of the Hebrews.

We followed the bank of the Salt Sea to its opening where the Jordan River feeds it. The river was rushing past us. Naomi explained that the river was swollen because it was the beginning of the barley harvest.

Standing before the river, I felt a sadness come over me. Would I ever cross this river again? I prepared to look behind me and take one last gaze toward the fields of Moab, but Naomi grabbed hold of my neck. "Do not look back," she said, "Now there is no looking back. Once a woman turned to salt for that." I remembered my father's story about the wife who turned her face toward the blazing cities and became a pillar of salt. So I looked ahead to the golden hills stretching before me.

I took Naomi's hand. "I am ready," I told her. We set our feet on the rocks of the Jordan until we felt only water and then swam until we felt rocks again. As we crossed, I felt the oil of the Salt Sea, the dust of the road, the sadness of Mahlon's death, and my life in the fields fall away into the water.

Day 4: The Road to Ephrath
Neither of us could rest that night, so we began the ascent from the Jordan River Valley up the Judean Hills. As we climbed the steepest hill, I asked, "El Shaddai, are you with me?" "She is with you," Naomi answered.

In the light of morning, Naomi's excitement became apparent. She began to speak rapidly. "By the afternoon, we will be in Bethlehem. It is harvest time so the fields will be bursting with life. Bethlehem is a place of happiness. My home. We're so close. We just need to follow the road."

"Naomi, will they recognize you?"

"They will remember me," she answered.

When the road began to flatten, Naomi turned to me. "You are tired, my daughter, we will rest at the tomb of Rachel." In the shade of some palms by Rachel's grave, Naomi told me of the great love shared by Rachel and Jacob and how Rachel's father tricked Jacob by giving him the eldest daughter and making him work seven more years for Rachel. She told me of Rachel's barrenness and how she finally gave birth to a famous dreamer. Naomi explained how Rachel left her home on the other side of the Jordan to follow Jacob to his land. "Rachel was strong like you," Naomi said, "she did not make it to Bethlehem, but you will."

I made my own promise to the spirit of Rachel that I would complete her journey and make it to Bethlehem. Then I looked at Naomi and made another promise to myself to take care of her. A Bedouin woman approached and gave us water to drink. She gave me a long look and a smile. "Bethlehem," she said pointing down the road. "My Bethlehem," Naomi said to me. I wondered what Naomi's people would think about her returning with a Moabite in place of her husband and sons. After drinking, Naomi stood up, faced Bethlehem and said, "I am ready." She took my hand and we walked the rest of the way to the city gates.

THE KINSMAN

Chapter one closes as the two women arrive in Bethlehem "at the beginning of the barley harvest." The harvest gives physical proof of

God's return and promises a similar restoration in Ruth's and Naomi's lives. As Naomi is greeted by the women of Bethlehem, she is given another forum to articulate her grief. While the female chorus fills the space left by Orpah, Naomi's diction is different from that on the road to return. Among her kinswomen, Naomi emphasizes that God has afflicted her. She has returned home, but must now face what such a return means.

The conversation between Naomi and the women is a completion of the one begun on the road to return. Naomi speaks of her pain and is reinducted into the community. Ruth and Naomi settle in the town of Bethlehem as the barley matures in the fields. In *Seasons of Our Joy,* Arthur Waskow describes the barley harvest:

> Barley is the quickest ripening grain and the most fertile–and so it was the quintessence of the fruitfulness of the land. The barley crop came to ripeness early in the spring–during or just after Pesach. Late in the spring–fifty days later–the wheat crop was ready.[16]

Ruth's situation corresponds with the barley harvest. A stranger to Bethlehem, she must adjust rapidly, or "ripen" to a new way of life. The bountiful harvest assures Ruth and Naomi that they have reached fields able to sustain them. Fifty days later, in these same fields, Ruth reconfronts her sexuality.

Chapter two begins with an announcement of Boaz's existence. "Now Naomi had a kinsman on her husband's side, a well-to-do man of the family of Elimelech; his name was Boaz" (2:1). This relative and his virtue are introduced before he actually enters the story. With mention of the spring harvest comes the vision of young men reaping the crops followed by women who gather them. As well as being the place where humanity comes into contact with the divine, the fields represent an environment of sexual openness and miraculous events. Outside of the community proper, the fields allow for actions unhindered by social codes.

Throughout the Bible, fields are associated with the fantastic. Cain invites Abel "to the field" where he attacks and murders him. Isaac first beholds Rebekah "in the field" where he has gone hoping either to meet her caravan, or to relieve himself. Reuben, Leah's son, finds the magical mandrakes "in the field" during harvest. It is "in the field" where an unnamed director steers Joseph toward his brothers. Like Cain, Joseph's brothers believe that they can harm their brother in an open space without ramifications. In the fields of Moab, Balaam's donkey perceives an angel and strays from the road. When Balaam beats his animal, she speaks to him and reveals the angel's presence (Num. 22:23). An angel of God visits Samson's mother "who was sitting in the fields; her husband was not with her" (Jud. 13:9). When the paranoid King Saul schemes against David's life, David seeks refuge in the fields. Jonathan meets him, reveals his father's pledge, and the two men "kiss one another," "shed tears together," and make an eternal pledge to each other (I Sam. 20:42).

Going "to the field" is an exploration of the unknown. In the case of Cain and Joseph's brothers, suppressed violence is released. Reuben's discovery of the mandrakes is the key to Rachel's fertility. Both Balaam and Samson's mother encounter God in the open spaces. In Isaac's and Jonathan's case, the fields are the place where their desires are satisfied. The mystery of fields lies at the base of Ruth's story.

The labor of harvesting was organized along clear social stratifications. Prominent landowners such as Boaz would oversee the work in the fields and hire men to plant and reap the crops. The workers in Boaz's fields are well treated, as evidenced by the hut provided for rest and the tent for meals. Boaz establishes places of refuge during the hot days of harvest. Such considerations may lend to his title of "a well-to-do man."

A more extensive hierarchy becomes evident through the character of "the young man in charge of the reapers." When Boaz first appears in his fields, he questions the young man about the appearance of Ruth, a new woman gathering in his fields. This "manager of the reapers" also serves as Boaz's advisor and confident. Beneath the reapers in the hierarchy are the gatherers, unmarried or poor women who support themselves by collecting the stalks which fall from the sheaves. The gatherers' vulnerability to the advances of male workers is apparent in Boaz's charge "that the young men not touch" Ruth. While the other gatherers are not insured the same protection, it seems that all the women in the fields do enjoy a unique independence. Although they are disenfranchised, the gatherers have the right to go to the fields, work, and support themselves.

Ruth continues her commitment to Naomi's survival. She turns to her mother-in-law and asks her permission to go and glean in the fields. Ruth's familiarity with the system of charity is apparent in her diction: "May I go out to the cornfields and glean behind anyone who will grant me favor?" Ruth knows that a young woman must find favor in the eyes of a field worker to ensure her success. Ruth says that she intends to gather "behind" someone, indicating that the reapers and gatherers negotiate their own agreements. Well aware of which attributes will work in her favor, Ruth tries her luck in the fields.

Since chapter two begins with the announcement of Boaz, Naomi's wealthy relative, we wonder to what extent Ruth is steered in his direction. Since the readers are introduced to Boaz before he actually appears, we assume that Ruth has received prior information. Boaz is called *Ish Gibbor Hayil* (a man of substance) which shows his importance and commitment to the community. He is the type of man which Elimelech failed to be. Yet it is the narrator, not Naomi, who asserts the connection. Naomi says simply, "Go, my daughter," encouraging Ruth to pursue a new challenge.

Ruth's request of permission shows her continued respect for her mother-in-law. Acting as an extension of Naomi, Ruth seeks her consent and makes sure that she is prepared to watch Ruth go out on her own. Ruth's trip to the fields is, in a sense, her leaving of the nest. Naomi agrees to Ruth's venture and calls her, "my daughter," indicating that their relationship is no longer defined by the deceased Mahlon. Ruth, like a daughter, holds Naomi's primary affection.

In her second act of autonomy, Ruth goes out to the fields. Her motion is described with three unmodified verbs, "and she went, and came, and gleaned." "As chance would have it," Ruth arrives in a field belonging to Boaz, who the narrator reminds us, is related to Elimelech. Suddenly, Boaz himself appears on the horizon. Polite and enthusiastic, he greets his workers: "The Lord be with you. And they answered him, the Lord, bless thee" (Ruth 2:4). The pleasant rapport between Boaz and his men confirms that God has returned to the fields. In the book of Ruth, God is not portrayed as a guiding voice or an elusive companion. Instead, the presence of God is to be found in the fields bursting with life and the kindness displayed by people. Once Ruth and Naomi return to Bethlehem, there is no separation between the figure of God and the people's daily lives. Divinity is an inherent part of a cohesive community.

After delivering his blessing, Boaz surveys his fields. Ruth catches his eye and Boaz asks the young man in charge of the reapers, "Whose girl is this?" Boaz may be asking behind whom Ruth is gleaning or who has staked a claim on the Moabite woman's affections. Ruth's supposition that she would glean after someone whose favor she won holds true. The young man in charge of the reapers is in possession of Ruth's entire story and relays it to Boaz:

She is a Moabite girl who has just come back with Naomi from the Moabite country. She asked if she might glean and gather among the swathes behind the reapers. She came and has been on her feet with hardly a moments rest (in the house) from daybreak till now (Ruth 2:6-8).

The young man in charge imparts Boaz with Ruth's background as well as her actions on that very day. With a sense of awe, he describes Ruth's graceful approach. The young man lauds Ruth's work by telling Boaz that she has hardly paused to take a breath. To the men working in the fields, Ruth is a wondrously curious figure. Boaz's manager anxiously tells him everything he knows about Ruth, eager to see how the landowner will respond to the Moabite woman.

The dialogue between Boaz and his advisor frames that of Boaz and Ruth. Ruth's association with Naomi may remind Boaz of his obligations as a kinsman to Naomi. He also possesses a piece of land which belonged to Naomi's late husband. Since Ruth is acting on Naomi's behalf, Boaz must treat her as he would his older relative. After learning her story, Boaz addresses Ruth who appears to be in close proximity: "Listen to me, my daughter: do not go and glean in any other field, and do not look any further, but keep close to my girls" (2:8). At their first meeting, Boaz calls Ruth "my daughter," the same endearment used by Naomi to send Ruth off. He tells her to wander no further, for she will be provided for in his fields. Boaz's offer of generosity also serves as a subtle command. As a test of her fidelity, he tells Ruth to stay in his fields alongside his maidens.

The request that Ruth remain in his field is charged with attraction. Boaz tells her to stay by his girls and not to play the field: "Watch where the men reap, and follow the gleaners; I have given them orders not to molest you. If you are thirsty, go and drink from the jars the men have filled" (2:9). Boaz instructs Ruth to keep her eyes on the field, not on the reapers. On his part, he will do everything he can to protect Ruth from the fields' rampant sexuality. Her behavior will prove to him what kind of woman she is.

Ruth lowers her face as a sign of gratitude and faces the land which she has claimed as her own. She responds to Boaz with an appreciation laced with suspicion. "Why have I found favour in thy eyes, that thou shouldst take notice of me, seeing I am a stranger?" (2:10). By asking him why he is extending himself, Ruth may be evading the attraction which she senses in Boaz's offer. Since a discussion regarding Naomi's land may have occurred on the road to return, Ruth might well understand Boaz's motivation. In any case, she responds with humility and grace.

Boaz attests to the power of oral transmission by telling Ruth that he respects her because of what he has heard: "Boaz answered, 'They have told me all that you have done for you mother-in-law since your husband's death, how you left your father and mother and the land of your birth, and came to a people you did not know before" (2:11). Impressed with Ruth, Boaz rolls out his red carpet and welcomes her to his land. In response to her query of why Boaz would treat a stranger so well, he explains that he wants to help her because she is a stranger. Boaz admires the risk which Ruth has taken in accompanying Naomi. Like Naomi, Boaz blesses Ruth by wishing her God's care: "The Lord reward your deed; may the Lord the God of Israel, under whose wings you have come to take refuge, give you all that you deserve" (2:12). The image of God spreading his wings is prevalent in biblical narrative (see Deut. 32:11; Ps. 36:8; 57:2; 61:5; 91:4), and echoes Ruth's promise to Naomi that "your God (is) my God." As Ruth has shown Naomi and will reveal to Boaz, she sees through the invocation of God. Ruth does not passively wait for God's assistance, but takes matters into her own hands. As she sees it, God has little to do with her immediate survival.

In response to Boaz, Ruth exerts power and sets her boundaries: "'Indeed sir,' she said, 'you have eased my mind and spoken kindly to me; may I ask you as a favor not to treat me only as one of your slave-girls?'" (2:13). Ruth accepts Boaz's courtesy, but lets him know that she will not behave as a slave-girl. She shows Boaz her understanding of field dynamics and resists his attempt to classify her with "his" other maidens. Boaz cannot claim her as part of his property or try to include her in his harem. This is the first of Ruth's rhetorical plays in which she asserts her own opinions while seeming to conform with other people's agendas. She thanks Boaz while letting him know where her gratitude stops. One midrashic storyteller imagines Boaz's response: "Heaven forfend, thou art not as one of the handmaidens (Amahoth), but as one of the matriarchs (Imahoth)."[17] Another expands Boaz's praise even more: "He said: you are to be very important and your sons will be the leaders of Israel and you will wear the royal crown."[18]

Boaz continues his hospitable overtures by inviting Ruth to have lunch with him and his men. "When meal-time came round, Boaz said to her, 'Come here and have something to eat, and dip your bread in the sour wine.' So she sat beside the reapers, and he passed her some roasted grain" (2:14). Ruth sits among the men as a guest of honor. In the same manner that Ruth's pledge to Naomi allowed her to overcome cultural boundaries, her clever response to Boaz enables her to transcend the social hierarchy. Ruth does not exploit her privilege; she eats and then returns to her work. "She ate all she wanted and still had some left over. When she got up to glean, Boaz gave the men orders. 'She,' he said, 'may glean even among the sheaves; do not scold her. or you may even pull out some corn from the bundles and leave it for her to glean, without reproving her'" (2:15-16). Ruth makes a lasting impression on Boaz. As she leaves, Boaz speaks of her to the reapers and ensures her success. With a good deal of tenderness, he tells his men to give Ruth special treatment. He wants to feel that he has done everything in his power to ease her adjustment. Boaz's attention and flirtation lends intrigue to Ruth's first day in the fields.

RUTH THE MOABITE

Joseph Campbell conjures *The Hero With a Thousand Faces*, the man who appears as savior to the world in stories throughout the ages. He speaks of the hero as Arthur, Buddha, and Skywalker, men whose journeys follow a principle cycle which turns with equal power in the individual psyche. Campbell defines the three primary steps of the journey as departure, initiation, and return. Movement through these stages is possible only through the hero's acceptance of challenge. Ruth is such a hero who passes three distinct tests on her way to return.

In Naomi's lament, Ruth hears a call to adventure which enables her to renounce a previous life. Separation from the past gives the hero the power of self-definition. When Ruth leaves Moab, she departs from a familiar framework and embarks on an independent journey. Her first test, the crossing of the desert, allows her the time to recreate herself. When she arrives in Bethlehem, she becomes Ruth the Moabite, a distinct and enigmatic figure. In a strange environment, Ruth is culturally defined. Instead of falling into the categorization, Ruth expands the definition to suit her. As her actions disprove Israelite preconceptions of Moabites, "the Moabite" becomes an indicator of her heroism.

Gathering the grain of the fields is Ruth's initiation into the community of Bethlehem. She passes the test of assimilation while permeating a male hierarchy. Ruth goes to the fields, a location outside of the community in order to gain acceptance into the community. Again, Ruth steps outside of category. When Boaz approaches Ruth in the fields, he offers her a working position in his harem. Ruth thanks Boaz for the attention, but asks him "not to treat (her) only as one of your slave-girls." Ruth continues to define herself and prove her value through action. By living with Naomi and laboring with the reapers, Ruth becomes a part of both the male and female sectors of Bethlehem. Being a stranger allows her to bridge the gender gap.

Before the movement from life to death can be completed, Ruth must cross an internal desert. She must take off her hero's armor and confront her sexuality. Again Naomi provides the call to action, instructing Ruth to "wash and anoint yourself, put on your cloak and go down to the threshing-floor." As in the passage from Moab to Bethlehem, Ruth's descent to the threshing-floor is an act of self-definition. Ruth approaches Boaz like a prostitute, but leaves him having secured his promise of marriage. She is at once prostitute and matriarch. When Ruth gives birth to Obed, the return to life is completed.

Although Ruth successfully completes the journey from death to life, there is no indication of her transformation. We do not know how, or if, her tests alter her. While Naomi's return from bitterness is explicit, nothing is mentioned about the changes undergone by Ruth. At all stages of her adventure, Ruth is able to use skillful rhetoric to divert attention from her desires and opinions. After she completes her task, Ruth disappears from the story and Naomi steps into the position of mother. The omission of Ruth's future corresponds with the omission of her past. Ruth, defined entirely by action, is a character of constant present.

Never physically described, Ruth's age, stature, and appearance remain a mystery. Ruth the Moabite is a faceless hero. Because she is not said to be beautiful, her beauty never becomes an issue. If we believe that Ruth is striking, it is because we want her to be and if, like Elizabeth Cady Stanton, we envision Ruth as "neither rich nor beautiful, but a poor stranger," it is the imposition of another romantic standard. As a hero, Ruth rescues women from patriarchal scrutiny as much as she saves Naomi from anguish. Her facelessness allows a break from a tradition which equated women's value with their beauty.

Throughout the Hebrew Bible, women who look good are good. Abraham admits to his wife Sarah, "I know very well that you are a beautiful woman" (Gen. 12:12). Of Rebekah, the narrators assure us, "the girl was very beautiful, a virgin, who had had no intercourse with a man" (Gen. 24:16). Rachel is considered superior to her sister because "Leah was dull-eyed, but Rachel was graceful and beautiful" (Gen. 29:18). When David spots Bathsheba from the palace roof, he cannot repress his desire because "she was so very beautiful" (2 Samuel 11:2). By never physically describing Ruth, the narrator introduces a new kind of female glory. Her value is appraised according to a feminine standard. Ruth liberates biblical heroines from the beauty myth.

In place of a physical description, Ruth is called "the Moabite," an epithet holding definitive historical connotations. Moabite women were known for their beauty and forbidden lure. The book of Numbers speaks of when "the people began to commit whoredom with the daughters of Moab" (Num. 25:1). In a midrashic passage, the techniques of seduction are described: "Would you like a glass of wine? And when he drinks it, the Ṣirṣur awakens his desire (Ṣirṣur is herbs mixed with wine used to increase desire). They write on their flesh the name of impurity and sit naked and he who sees them burns with desire."[19]

Calling her "Ruth the Moabite" may have indicated a certain kind of beauty in the same way that the phrases "French woman" or "California girl" operate as descriptions. For ancient audiences, the title "Ruth the Moabite" may have provided insight into her appearance and character. Perhaps the title is so often repeated because the character of Ruth redefines the characterization of Moabite women. Adele Berlin perceives the assertion of culture which is six times repeated as revealing the importance of origin.

> In the ancient world there was no mechanism for religious conversion or change of citizenship; the very notion was unthinkable. Religion and peoplehood defined one's ethnic identity, and this could no more be changed than could the color of one's skin. A Moabite was always a Moabite, wherever he or she lived.[20]

Thus Ruth is a Moabite in the same manner that Elimelech was "a man from Bethlehem in Judah" even in the midst of his flight. The difference is that Ruth adapts to life in Bethlehem while retaining a separateness. She never ceases to be a Moabite, instead she changes what being called a Moabite means. Through her unique independence, Ruth makes "the Moabite," the tag of a hero.

TRANSFERENCE

Ruth works in Boaz's fields until evening. Her departure at the end of day proves her endurance and recalls that evening is the customary time of female assembly. During the transitional hours, she can easily travel from the fields to her mother-in-law's house. Ruth has remained close to the other gatherers and accompanies them back to town.

In a three verb sequence, Ruth leaves the fields, arrives at Naomi's house, and sets out the fruit of her labors. She disproves Naomi's lament of emptiness by offering her the "bushel of barley" which she has gathered. By transferring the substance of the fields to her mother-in-law, Ruth becomes the medium through which Naomi is reconnected with her land and her God. The presentation of barley which symbolizes the earth's rejuvenative power is Ruth's first fertility offering. As if to a deity, Ruth surrenders her rewards. The quality of hesed, or transcendent kindness, shows through.

Ruth performed her first act of *hesed* by giving Naomi a reason to live. The intensity of her pledge served as a form of resuscitation necessary to shock Naomi into a recognition of her own worth. The presentation of barley, a continuation of the pledge, sustains Naomi on a long term basis. Ruth ensures Naomi's spiritual nourishment by providing her with crops grown in the fields from which she has been long separated. Ruth's actions restore Naomi to her native land and reveal that God has returned to Bethlehem. The second act of *hesed* is "filling" Naomi with the products of a bountiful harvest.

To vary her sacrifice, Ruth brings "out what she had saved from her meal and gave it to her." Even when eating with the owner of the fields, Ruth thinks of Naomi. Without mentioning her industriousness or Boaz's special treatment, Ruth gives Naomi leftovers from the meal. Naomi fails to recognize Ruth's personal power and blesses "the man" who bestowed the gifts. Naomi hungers for the story behind the barley. "Where did you glean today? Which way did you go? Blessings on the man who kindly took notice of you" (2:19). The abundance of food is attributed to the man who "took notice" of Ruth. Naomi's response to the gift illustrates their generational differences. Where Ruth looks inward, Naomi looks to a male figure for security and a male God for redemption. Naomi's autonomy is a reaction to unexpected circumstance, while Ruth has chosen her independence. For Naomi a redeemer represents survival, while to Ruth, a redeemer is only the vehicle to make Naomi happy.

Ruth relates the day's activities and describes Boaz's fields. The notion flashes in Naomi's mind: A perfect match! Instantly she invokes the name of God. "'Blessings on him from the Lord,' said Naomi. 'The Lord has kept faith with the living and the dead. For this man is related to us and is our next-of-kin'" (2:20). Naomi misses the point again and blesses God while not thanking or acknowledging Ruth. The only survivor of her family, Naomi perceives herself as one "of the dead." Mention of Boaz leads her to believe that perhaps God has not altogether forgotten her. In Ruth's meeting with the kinsman, Naomi perceives the hand of God.

Since it is so well woven in the story, it is hard to discern when Naomi's conspiracy begins. She may have targeted Boaz as a possible redeemer during the silent journey or when Ruth made her request to go to the fields. Naomi plans on getting more than barley from Boaz. Since Boaz possesses a plot of land belonging to Naomi, the bushel of barley is Naomi's first taste of home. When she eats, Naomi partakes of God's blessing. This food brings her back to life, or back to a life which she has previously known.

As she continues her report, Ruth alters the events. She plays her second rhetorical trick by changing Boaz's words: "'And what is more,' said Ruth the Moabitess, 'he told me to stay close to his men until they had finished all his harvest'" (2:21). Boaz, however, told her to "keep close to his girls." Is this Ruth's ploy to shock Naomi into recognizing her independence? Does she want Naomi to be aware of the fact that by going to the fields she has crossed a gender boundary? Perhaps Ruth is uncomfortable with Naomi's plot and does not want Naomi to start matchmaking. The idea of associating with the other girls may neutralize Ruth's sense of personal valor.

Ruth does not admit to the sexual nature of her dialogue with Boaz. Not addressing what it means to be one of "Boaz's girls," she changes the story to deny the sexual undertones. Perhaps Ruth does not want to reveal the attraction to Naomi, her primary love. A description of the fecund fields would only intensify Naomi's loneliness. Ruth tries to stick to practical details and avoid talk of kinsmen and remarriage. Naomi is steadfast. She reminds Ruth of how the charity system operates by reiterating Boaz's advice: "It is best for you, my daughter," Naomi answered "to go out with his girls; let no one catch you in another field" (2:22). She outlines the hierarchy of the fields and advises Ruth to keep company with other women. As in gatherings by the well, women would go to the fields in groups to avoid harassment. A euphemism for promiscuity, Naomi tells Ruth not to meet the young men in any field other than the one where they labor. In a motherly tone, Naomi advises Ruth on proper conduct.

By the end of the second chapter, Ruth has mastered life in Bethlehem. Abiding by Naomi's words, Ruth remains close to his girls, "gleaning with them till the end of both barley and wheat harvests; but she lived with her mother-in-law" (2:23). The verb used for Ruth's proximity to the other women is *Tidbaq* which has the same root *(DBQ)* as *Dabqa*, the verb used to describe Ruth's "clinging" to Naomi on the road to return. This verb is an indicator of a closeness particular to female relationships.

As chapter one ended with the barley harvest, chapter two ends with the harvest of wheat. Ruth has passed her second test: the acquisition of food. In the time between the two harvests, Ruth adjusts to her new situation. The crops become the wings which shelter Ruth and her work becomes a form of worship. She establishes herself as a notable community member by living with Naomi and not meeting with any men in the darkened fields.

Although the period between the barley and wheat harvests is about fifty days, nothing more is said of the interactions between Ruth and Boaz. After their charged meeting, are we to assume that they make no further contact? Do the two not meet, or does Boaz not extend himself? Does Boaz avoid Ruth because he is aware of his redemptive responsibilities? In terms of narrative time, their meeting and consummation seems rapid, yet it actually spans several months.

We do not know if the two speak or even exchange knowing glances. Nothing moves until Ruth takes further initiative.

THE THRESHING FLOOR

As spring deepens and the fields bloom with wheat, Ruth faces her third test. Naomi introduces thoughts of a more permanent assimilation: "My daughter, I want to see you happily settled" (Ruth 3:1). With a rhetorical question, Naomi initiates the next phase in the movement toward life. She speaks of a different lifestyle which will be more restful and stable, then steers Ruth toward the very field whose avoidance she had originally advised.

As Ruth sought to revitalize Naomi with her pledge and food offering, Naomi pushes Ruth toward a sexual reawakening. It is unclear, however, if Naomi seeks a home and comfort for Ruth, or for herself. Recalling her initial blessing, Naomi speaks to Ruth of finding the "rest which will do her well." In other words, Naomi would like to see her "in the house of a husband." Ruth has proved that she can labor and can take care of herself. Naomi, in turn, presents another challenge. "Now there is our kinsman Boaz; you were with his girls. Tonight he is winnowing barley at the threshing floor" (3:2-3). Directing Ruth toward her relative, Naomi presents the facts blatantly. She knows where Boaz will be and what he will be doing. Although Naomi has not been to the fields, she is aware of the activities of a harvest night. Perhaps she remembers and romanticizes her own such nights. Boaz may be winnowing the barley of Naomi's fields and Ruth is sent as a representative of Naomi's claim. Her visit serves as a profound reminder of Boaz's responsibility. Naomi's knowledge of Boaz's whereabouts and her direction is proof of her conspiracy. She intends to reclaim her land.

Naomi tells Ruth how to dress and how to approach: "Wash, anoint yourself, put on your cloak and go down to the threshing floor," she begins, echoing the instructions God gave Moses at Mt. Sinai: "Go to the people, and sanctify them today and tomorrow. And let them wash their clothes, and be ready ... for on the third day the Lord will come down in the sight of all the people upon Mount Sinai" (Ex. 19:10). Ruth and the people of Israel both undergo a period of cleansing before meeting with a sublimated force. The people of Israel, estranged from their God, are transformed by the meeting at Sinai. In preparation for the encounter, they must cleanse themselves of the past as well as the dust of foreign soil. When God speaks the ten commandments, the union between the people and their God is solidified. The commandments offer a stability to the people similar to that which Boaz gives Ruth. Naomi creates a ritual in which Ruth cleanses herself of the past. When Ruth anoints herself, she washes away her life as a pagan, a wife, and a laborer. Approaching Boaz,

Ruth confronts a sublimated sexuality. The meeting transforms her and changes the course of her life.

Concealed beneath her coat, Ruth makes her way to the threshing floor with Naomi's words ringing in her head: "Go down to the threshing-floor, but do not make yourself known to the man until he has finished eating and drinking. But when he lies down, take note of the place where he lies. Then go in, turn back the covering at his feet and lie down" (3:3-4). As Naomi has kept her agenda hidden, she advises Ruth to act first and make requests later. Ruth is to approach Boaz after he is well fed and at least a little drunk, then lie beside him in the makeshift bed. Naomi explains that timing is everything. The balance of approach and concealment in Ruth's seduction resembles that of Judith and Esther, the other two women for whom biblical and post-biblical books are named.

Located in the fields, the threshing floor is a place where overt sexuality is permissible, and welcomed. Ruth must employ different virtues than those exhibited on her first approach to the fields. But like the initial movement, she must adapt to a new set of codes and customs. Like an alien, she enters an unexplored environment. The threshing floor must have been wild after a bountiful harvest drew to a close, with the reapers jubilant, relaxed, and eager for visits.

Encouraging her to take sexual initiative, Naomi comes close to recommending prostitution. She explains to her Moabite daughter-in-law how to prepare herself, how to approach, and what to do. Francine Klagsbrun points out: "Naomi guides Ruth in the ways of a woman with a man, teaching her how to dress and speak, how to be coy and seductive, how to seek a husband, almost as if Ruth has never before been wed, let alone to Naomi's son."[21] Naomi steers Ruth directly to Boaz's genitals. The verb GLH means to reveal or expose nakedness [Lev. 18:6-19; 20:11; Isa. 47:2; Ezek. 16:36; 22:10]. The noun *mar-ge-lo-tav*, can be interpreted as the place of his feet as in the following verse: "... and his feet like in color to polished brass" (Dan. 10:6). Or as it is found in other stories: "in the same day shall the Lord save ... and the hair of the feet" (Isa. 7:20) or in the verse: "... surely he covereth his feet in his summer chamber" (Jud. 3:24). "Since the term 'foot' is a common enough biblical euphemism for 'penis,' the difference in Hebrew between 'uncover his feet' and 'uncover his foot [=penis]' is subtle. In this context, and with an appropriate hesitation after 'uncover,' could Ruth (or a reader) miss the sexual intent implicit in Naomi's instruction?"[22]

Naomi concludes her lesson by handing the reins to Boaz. "He will tell you what to do," she says to Ruth.

With a word play, Ruth reverses Naomi's prioritization of men. She accepts Naomi's mission by telling her, "I will do whatever you tell me." Ruth agrees to seduce Boaz, but only because Naomi has asked it of her. Since the vow of lifetime commitment has been made to Naomi, Ruth unites with Boaz only to "fill" Naomi's emptiness. Ruth's affiliation is clear. No matter who she lies beside, her primary love is Naomi.

Ruth does not falter in the execution of Naomi's plan. She moves through the night anointed and wearing her best. By going down to the threshing floor, Ruth crosses a clearly delineated gender boundary. From her mother-in-law's house where she has been leading a life of chastity, Ruth enters a male domain. For Naomi, Ruth has transcended cultural barriers. For Boaz, in the name of Naomi, Ruth overcomes gender separation.

> So she went down to the threshing-floor and did exactly as her mother-in-law had told her. When Boaz had eaten and drunk, he felt at peace with the world and went to lie down at the far end of the heap of grain. She came in quietly, turned back the covering at his feet and lay down (3:6-8).

Ruth waits in the shadows until the right moment. Boaz is "at peace with the world" after the customary feasting and selects his place among the grain. Ruth slips next to him among the harvested crops. The suspense builds as the soon-to-be lovers lie together on the open roofed threshing floor. The idyllic image is reminiscent of Eden and seems the perfect beginning of a partnership.

In the middle of the night or in the middle of their night, Boaz realizes that a woman is beside him. He asks, "Who are you?" Disguised as a simple request of identity, Boaz desires that Ruth reveal herself completely. He wants to know her agenda and what she wants from him. As the female chorus gave Naomi the forum, Boaz allows Ruth to tell her story. An ice-breaking tactic, the question precludes the identification of other desires. In a beautiful midrashic passage, Boaz asks Ruth if she is human or divine:

> She clung to him like ivy, and he began to finger her hair. "Spirits have no hair," he thought, so he said, "Who art thou? a woman or a spirit?" She answered, "A woman." "A maiden or a married woman?" She answered, "A maiden." "Art thou clean or unclean?" She answered, "Clean." And behold a woman, purest of women, lay at his feet. [23]

During these moments of intimacy, Ruth has a chance to define herself as more than a Moabite. The Aramaic translation of *Ruth* offers a more prudish interpretation in which Boaz is paralyzed by fear: "The man was perplexed and trembled. His body became soft like a turnip and he saw a woman all bent down at his feet. He suppressed his passion and did not conjoin." [24] In this passage, Boaz must protect his chastity from the seductive Moabitess. Paralyzed by anxiety and fear, the midrashic Boaz becomes "soft like a turnip" and cannot participate in love making. This Boaz who suppresses his passion is quite dissimilar from the biblical Boaz who presses Ruth to stay the night. In the biblical story, Boaz and Ruth spend the night together, but rise before the sun to avoid gossip. Their first night is devoted to revealing their identities and taking off their clothes.

Ruth, in fine rhetorical form, answers Boaz's question of who she is with a word play. Her response defies Naomi's direction. Where Naomi told Ruth to wait passively for Boaz to tell her what to do, Ruth informs Boaz what she wants him to do. "'I am your servant, Ruth,' she replied 'Now spread your skirt (wings) over your servant, because you are my next-of-kin'" (3:9-10). On their first meeting, Boaz wished Ruth the reward of "the Lord the God of Israel, under whose wings you have come to take refuge." Ruth informs Boaz, in turn, that she wants comfort beneath his wings and commands him to spread them over her. As she has shown Naomi, Ruth reminds Boaz that change requires human action. The image of Boaz spreading his wings over Ruth while God blesses them with the harvest calls to mind spring fertility rites. The passion shared by Ruth and Boaz reflects the abundance of their surroundings. By referencing Boaz's previous blessing, Ruth makes her night with him an extension of the blessing.

Boaz, mildly missing the point, evokes God. "The Lord has blessed you, my daughter. This last proof of your loyalty is greater than the first; you have not sought after any young man, rich or poor" (3:10-11). From Boaz's perspective, Ruth's last proof of loyalty (curling up next to him) is greater than her first (accompanying Naomi to Bethlehem). He admits that he used the days between the barley and wheat harvests as a period of testing. As God tested the people for forty nine days in the desert before giving them the Torah, Boaz observed Ruth's actions in the fields. She proved herself by working hard and not seeking the company of any young man. By "proving her loyalty" to Boaz, Ruth passes her third test. She has journeyed to a foreign country, harvested the fruits of the land, and gotten her man.

Pleased by her presence, Boaz assuages Ruth's anxieties. "Set your mind at rest, my daughter. I will do whatever you ask; for, as the whole neighborhood knows, you are a capable woman" (3:11). Boaz accepts the role of redeemer and pledges to do whatever Ruth requests. His promise fulfills the triangular relationship. Naomi told Ruth to do whatever Boaz told her, Ruth told Naomi that she would do whatever she said, and Boaz has agreed to do whatever Ruth asks. According to Boaz's report, Ruth's heroism is known throughout the community, and their marriage would be well received. Boaz complements Ruth through the lips of "the whole neighborhood."

Boaz's tone changes as the logistics of marriage cross his mind, "are you sure that I am the next-of-kin? There is a kinsman even closer than I," yet he resolves to leave such matters for the morning. "Spend the night here and then in the morning, if he is willing to act as your next-of-kin, well and good; but if he is not willing, I will do so; I swear it by the Lord. Now lie down till morning" (3:13-14). One thing of which Boaz is sure is that he wants Ruth to spend the night. He abandons marriage negotiations for sexual innuendo and passion. She opens his eyes to her wonders on the threshing room floor. Surrounded only by wheat, they are exposed to the night wind and air. Ruth and Boaz pass the night hours together, learning the curve of each other's bodies and the texture of each other's skin. Boaz learns of Ruth's other virtues; Ruth learns her second lover.

No matter how excited Boaz may be about Ruth's virtues, the law comes first. If the closest kin accepts his duty, Boaz vows to step aside. But if not, Boaz pledges himself to Ruth. She stays with him until dawn and rises "before one man could recognize another" to keep gossip at a minimum. Her seduction has been a success, yet the period of concealment is not over.

To avoid any blemish on their reputations, Boaz says, "It must not be known that a woman has been to the threshing-floor." Legal matters still need to be addressed. A prominent community member, Boaz has appearances to maintain. Ruth and Boaz share the secret of their night and the suspense of an unknown future.

Ruth is well rewarded for her visit. "Then he said, 'Bring me the cloak you have on, and hold it out.' So she held it out, and he put in six measures of barley and lifted it on her back, and she went to town" (3:15-16). Heavy with provisions, Ruth steals away from the threshing floor. The gift of barley lends to the image of Ruth as a prostitute. Perhaps the barley is evidence that Boaz is spreading his wings, for Ruth departs, "filled" on many counts.

One cannot help but imagine Ruth's walk home in the predawn hours. Carrying the barley, her thoughts run to her new lover. Will he keep his promise to act the kinsman's part? Will the third part of her journey secure her place in Bethlehem? Ripe with the secrets of night, Ruth returns to her mother-in-law's house. She stands at the door, and Naomi asks, "Who are you, my daughter?" the very question asked by Boaz. Why does Naomi ask after Ruth's identity? The use of "my daughter" shows that she is well aware of who Ruth is and desires other information. She wants to hear the night's story.

Ruth tells Naomi all "that the man did to her" and involves her in the story: "He gave me these six measures of barley," she said; "he would not let me come home to my mother-in-law empty-handed" (3:17). Ruth quotes Boaz as saying something which he has never actually said. In other words, she reframes the story to illustrate the extent to which her actions have "filled" her mother-in-law. With the inclusion of Naomi in the threshing floor dialogue, the triangular relationship is maintained. By making her mother-in-law present in the narrative, Ruth shows her overriding concern for Naomi's happiness. She focuses on Naomi's well being, not on her own excitement. She does not want talk of Boaz to diminish Naomi's sense of importance.

Naomi has the last word: "Wait, my daughter, until you see what will come of it. He will not rest until he has settled the matter today" (3:18). Like Boaz, Naomi recommends Ruth's patience and predicts that the man will fulfill his promise. Both the Bethlehemites ask the same questions and offer the same advice. Naomi seems confident that Boaz will perform the legalistic formalities. The conspiracy becomes apparent.

THE CITY GATES

As promised, the man does not rest. Chapter four begins with Boaz already at the city gate attending to the legalities of his relationship. The only other male scene beside the death of Elimelech and his sons, this scene at the gates reads like a parody. After spending the night with Ruth on the threshing floor, Boaz has vowed to do all that he can to be Ruth's redeemer. He goes to the city gate, the traditional locale of male assembly, and has a seat. As chance would have it, the man occupying the position of primary redeemer passes by. Boaz calls out: "'Hey there Mr. So and So, come and sit down.' He came and sat down. Then Boaz stopped ten elders of the town, and asked them to sit there, and they did so" (4:2) (ot). The name of the first redeemer is not given, either to conceal the man's identity or to lend humor to the depiction of legal negotiations. While the city gate is traditionally portrayed as the sight where important transactions occur, the formalities of this scene are inflated.

With an audience of Mr. So and So and the elders, Boaz states his case:

> You will remember the strip of field that belonged to our brother Elimelech. Naomi has returned from the Moabite country and is selling it. I promised to open the matter with you, to ask you to acquire it in the presence of those who sit here, in the presence of the elders of my people. If you are going to do your duty as next-of-kin, then do so, but if not, someone must do it. So tell me, and then I shall know; for I come after you as next-of-kin (4:3-5).

This is the first overt mention of the land which belongs to Naomi and is the basis of Ruth's and Boaz's relationship. Part of the fields, where Ruth gleaned, belong to Naomi. Thus the conspiracy to seduce Boaz is inextricable from a plot to reclaim the land. Why did the dialogue regarding Naomi's land not occur immediately after she returned home? The levirate marriage laws were not activated until Ruth put them into effect. Although such laws were established as safety nets for women whose husbands died, they are not immediately implemented. The patriarchal system only works for women who are willing to work the system and overstep its bounds. Male assembly around the issue of Naomi's land happens only because Boaz is motivated by Ruth's virtues.

Boaz employs a strategy of concealment and construction similar to Ruth's. By presenting the necessary information in increments, he hopes to achieve his end. He creates the image of Naomi selling her land, something which she is not in a position to do. Pleased with the easy acquisition of land, Mr. So and So accepts the kinsman's role: "He answered, 'I will act as next-of-kin'" (4:4). Boaz answers with a stipulation: "On the day when you acquire the field from Naomi, you also acquire Ruth the Moabitess, the dead man's wife so as to perpetuate the name of the dead man with his patrimony" (4:5). Boaz informs his competition that with the land comes the woman and the woman needs to have children in order to keep the family name alive. By speaking in the name of the law without betraying his emotions, he proves as skillful a rhetoritician as Ruth. When Mr. So and So learns of the marriage required for the acquisition of land, he backs down. "Thereupon the next-of-kin said, 'I cannot act myself, for I should risk losing my own patrimony. You must therefore do my duty as next-of-kin. I cannot act'" (4:7). The thought of marrying Ruth paralyzes the unnamed kinsman. We never know if Mr. So and So is already married, impotent, or fearful of marrying a Moabite. The midrash attributes his decision to racism. "He said: 'The former ones (Mahlon and Chilion) died only because they took them to wife;

shall I go and take her? Heaven forfend that I should take her; I will not contaminate my seed, I will not introduce a disqualification into my children.'"[25] Whatever the reason, Mr. So and So declines the offer and allows Boaz to fill his shoes. To seal the contract, Boaz and Mr. So and So switch sandals: "Now in those old days, when property was redeemed or exchanged, it was the custom for a man to pull off his sandal and give it to the other party. This was the form of attestation in Israel. So the next-of-kin said to Boaz, 'acquire it for yourself,' and pulled off his sandal" (4:7). The sandal switch stands out as a particularly strange incident. No such custom is recorded anywhere else in biblical literature. The narrator inflects, mockingly, that this is how transactions were conducted in the "old days" of judges judging. The disclaimer about archaic customs and the image of the two men swapping shoes adds to the humorous, pseudo-formality of the scene. We can contrast the quick decision made by Ruth to go to the fields with the elaborate procedure used by Boaz to gain redeemership. Male assembly is portrayed as overly rigid and bombastic. Like Ruth, Boaz must employ stealth to make the system work for him.

To finalize the agreement, Boaz articulates the conditions to the elders.

> You are witnesses today that I have acquired from Naomi all that belonged to Elimelech and all that belonged to Mahlon and Chilion; and, further, that I have myself acquired Ruth the Moabitess, wife of Mahlon, to be my wife, to perpetuate the name of the deceased with his patrimony, so that his name may not be missing among his kindred and at the gate of his native place. You are witnesses this day (4:9-10).

Although she is not present, Naomi acts a a silent partner in the transaction. She has filled the shoes of her dead husband, and it is from her that Boaz acquires property and a wife. Well aware of Naomi's agenda, Boaz says that the reason for the marriage is "to perpetuate the name of the deceased." This speech represents the culmination of Naomi's plot. Boaz's desire to include the name of the dead at the "gate of his native place," emphasizes the importance of community, even in the afterlife. Boaz wants to bring Elimelech, Mahlon, and Chilion back from their exile by giving birth to an heir.

Adele Berlin views Boaz's speech as the point where "the story comes full circle: the family that left its land and lost its male line has returned to its homeland and restored its male line and patrimony."[26] Presence at the "gate" represents union with community and God. By marrying Ruth, Boaz reintegrates the dead men into their community. He does his part to heal the broken family. The elders exonerate Boaz by blessing Ruth: "May the Lord make this woman, who has come to your home, like Rachel and Leah, the two who built up the house of Israel" (4:11). Startling in that the matriarchal line is referenced by Bethlehem's male leaders, this blessing is the final step in Ruth's naturalization.

As Rachel and Leah built the house of Israel together, Ruth's and Naomi's collective efforts give rise to a new era. For the first time, male characters acknowledge the matriarchal continuum. Ilana Pardes points out, "This is the only case in the Bible where matriarchs are called up from the past to serve as a model for the future 'building' of the house of Israel."[27] Although Rachel, the beloved, is mentioned first, the sisters are spoken of as a team, not as rivals. Ruth has followed the footsteps of Rachel and Leah in that she traveled to a foreign land to follow her love, but the elders hope that Ruth, like the two sisters, will give birth to men of substance. "Like Rachel and Leah, Ruth and Naomi abandon a land of idol worshipers. Like Rachel and Leah, Ruth and Naomi use courage and guile to achieve their ends in a world in which women have few options for surviving on their own. Like Rachel and Leah, Ruth and Naomi are driven to shape the destiny of their people."[28] Ruth's receiving of the primary blessing and the reference to Rachel and Leah as the "builders of the house of Israel" indicates the female narrator.

The elders continue their blessing. While the focus shifts to Boaz, female action remains the primary theme: "May you do great things in Ephrathah and keep a name alive in Bethlehem. May your house be like the house of Perez, whom Tamar bore to Judah, through the offspring the Lord will give you by this girl" (4:11-12). By transferring food, Ruth served as the medium between Naomi and God. In Boaz's case, Ruth is the medium of the patrilineal legacy. The importance of Ruth's actions are highlighted in the evocation of other female heroes. The elders cast her into the mold of other non-Israelite women who created the nation.

> The references to Rachel, Leah, and Tamar, then, not only serve to welcome Ruth into the Judean community by linking her with the mothers of that community; they also, and most especially, lead us to view her in the mold of the heroic women who preserved the people of Israel and ensured its continuity.[29]

With Ruth's heroism well established, she is ready to begin the matriarchal journey and follow in Rachel's and Leah's footsteps. Ruth marries Boaz, is visited by God, and conceives a child: "So Boaz took Ruth and made her his wife. When they came together, the Lord caused her to conceive and she bore Boaz a son" (4:13). After the exploration of her independence and a series of personal tests, Ruth "comes together" with the God evoked by Naomi and Boaz. Ruth gains the power of creation, bringing the narrative cycle full circle. Her efforts not only enrich Bethlehem, but also usher in the messianic period.

The Davidic dynasty stems from Ruth's union with Boaz and with God. The power of this union is expressed by R. Abahu:

> If a giant marries a giantess, what do they produce? Mighty men. Boaz married Ruth. Whom did they produce? David, of whom it is said,

skillful in playing, and a mighty man of valour and a man of war, and prudent in affairs, and a comely person and the Lord with him.[30]

After she conceives, Ruth disappears from the narrative. Her voice is replaced by the female chorus congratulating Naomi. Ruth and Boaz are not seen with their child; instead Naomi lays him on her lap and is praised for maternity. Picking up where the last conversation left off, the female chorus emphasizes Naomi's fulfillment: "Blessed be the Lord today, for he has not left you without a next-of-kin. May the dead man's name be kept alive in Israel" (Ruth 4:14). In the welcoming scene, Naomi spoke to the women of her bitterness. In the naming ceremony, they speak of Naomi's blessing and the fact that God "has not left" her. Like the men at the gate, the female chorus is concerned with preserving the name of the dead.

Boaz is praised by the "male chorus" and Naomi is blessed by the female one. Ruth is spoken of, but never spoken to: "The child will give you new life and cherish you in your old age; for your daughter-in-law who loves you, who has proved better to you than seven sons, has borne him" (4:15). Described in hyperbolic terms, Ruth is said to be better than seven sons. Seven being the number of good fortune, the chorus speaks to Naomi of inherently feminine values. Naomi has never spoken of Ruth, yet the chorus knows the whole story. Where the men need to grasp for similarities, the women speak in absolutes. "Better than seven sons" is a term of liberation. "Women have value," the chorus tells Naomi, "without men, just on their own." The chorus tells Naomi some things that she has forgotten. They point out Ruth's love.

As the blessing comes to a close, Naomi takes the child, lays him on her lap, and becomes his nurse. The grandmother claims the child. From Naomi's previous statement, "Am I likely to bear any more sons to be husbands for you?" we can assume that Naomi has passed menopause. It is impossible for her to nurse the infant. The "nursing" is a symbolic action indicating that the triangular relationship has become a square. Boaz takes care of Ruth, Ruth takes care of Naomi, Naomi takes care of Obed. *Hesed,* Ruth's primary virtue is infectious. From the fragments of a previous unit, Ruth and Naomi have created a new family.

To close Naomi's return to Bethlehem and Ruth's matriarchal journey, the female chorus conducts a naming ceremony. "Her neighbors gave him a name: 'Naomi has a son,' they said; 'We will call him Obed.'" (4:17) Naomi does not actually have a son. Like Sarah, Rachel, and Leah with the offspring of their maidservants, Naomi claims the child by proxy. Naomi has a son because Ruth has offered the child to her. A collective female voice names Obed which means to work in the fields, or to worship God. Obed is an extension of Ruth who is an extension of Naomi. The story ends with a brief genealogy to enforce the power of Ruth's legacy. "He was the father of Jesse, the father of David" (4:17). Ruth and Naomi's journey leads to the monarchy. Their story is not an isolated novella, but is a part of a larger, historical cycle. The book of Ruth provides an example of upholding the covenant. Through Ruth's loyalty, Naomi's wisdom, and Boaz's justice, a new period begins.

To reinforce the connection between Ruth and King David, the genealogy is lengthened and repeated. "This is the genealogy of Perez: Perez was the father of Hezron, Hezron of Ram, Ram of Amminadab, Amminadab of Nahshon, Nahshon of Salmon, Salmon of Boaz, Boaz of Obed, Obed of Jesse, and Jesse of David" (4:18-22). This genealogy distracts from the emphasis on Ruth's heroism made by the female chorus. It tells a different story. This list which traces the men between Perez and David speaks of male lineage and primogeniture. The tone differs from that of the story and seems like an editor's attempt to have the last word. It is the phrasing of such genealogies which concerned the men at the city gate interested in preserving patriarchal legitimacy and order. The same genealogy appears in Matthew 1:1-16 to illustrate the messianic line.

> Judah was the father of Perez and Zerah, whose mother was Tamar.
> Perez was the father of Hezron, Hezron was the father of Ram. Ram was
> the father of Amminadab, Amminadab the father of Nahshon, Nahshon
> the father of Salmon. Salmon was the father of Boaz whose mother was
> Rahab, Boaz was the father of Obed whose mother was Ruth. Obed was
> the father of Jesse, Jesse was the father of King David. David was the
> father of Solomon, whose mother has been the wife of Uriah ... Matthan
> the father of Jacob. Jacob was the father of Joseph the husband of Mary.
> It was of her that Jesus who is called the Messiah was born (Matthew
> 1:1-16).

An accepted way to prove historical legitimacy, the genealogy
serves as the bridge between the Old and New Testaments. Whether
or not they are constructed, chronicles of who begat whom distract
from the mythological aspects of the Bible. They assert a historical
basis by referring to other biblical stories. The irony is that the
stories to which they refer may be mythical, in which case,
genealogies are an intricate attempt to create truth from fiction.

Each generation has a story whose themes are woven into the past
and future. The book of Ruth's conclusion is reflected in *Matthew's*
beginning. Before she disappears, Ruth is visited by God who
"caused her to conceive and she bore Boaz a son" (Ruth 4:14). The
women of Bethlehem name the child, then heredity is explained.
Matthew begins with the genealogy, then describes Mary's
immaculate conception. Before Mary has known her husband, "she
was found with child through the power of the Holy Spirit" (Matthew
1:18). When Mary's husband seeks to divorce her and "expose her
to the law," an angel appears to him. Joseph is informed that Mary
carries a divine child who will "save his people from their sins"
(Matthew 1:21).

While in Ruth's case, it is ambiguous if she is impregnated by Boaz or by God, Mary's partner is clearly God. The story of Mary takes the matriarchal journey cycle one step further. Not only does the virgin mother encounter God before she conceives, she "knows" only God. As pieces of matriarchal stories are recycled in the story of Ruth, the book of Ruth informs the gospel. Ancient perceptions are reconsidered and reformulated as each generation tells the story of its heroes.

Notes

Chapter four: Fortune's Reversal

1. Pardes, Op. Cit., 99.
2. Campbell, J. *The Hero with a Thousand Faces.* Princeton University Press (1973) 40.
3. Ruth Rabbah 1:4.
4. Ruth Rabbah 2:5.
5. Van Dijk-Hemmes, F. "Ruth: A Product of Women's Culture" in *A Feminist Companion to Ruth,* Op. Cit. 134-139.
6. Campbell, J. Op. Cit., 383.
7. Ruth Rabbah 2:6.
8. Bal, Mieke "Heroism and Proper Names, or The Fruit of Analogy" in *A Feminist Companion to Ruth*, Op. Cit., 49.
9. Ruth Rabbah 2:5.
10. Canticles Rabbah.
11. Ruth Rabbah 2:11.
12. Targum Ruth 1:6.
13. Ruth Rabbah 2:12.
14. Pardes, Op. Cit., 71-72.
15. Pardes, 115.
16. Waskow, Arthur. *Seasons of Our Joy.* Bantam Books (New York, NY, 1982) 165.

17. Ruth Rabbah 5:5.

18. Yalkut Ruth, 603.

19. Shabazi, S. Hemdat Yamim for Balaq, 449.

20. Berlin, A. *Reading Ruth*, Op. Cit. 257-258.

21. Klagsbrun, F. "Ruth and Naomi, Rachel and Leah: Sisters Under the Skin" in *Reading Ruth*, Op. Cit., 261.

22. Rashkow, I. "Ruth: the Discourse of Power and the Power of Discourse" in *A Feminist Companion to Ruth*, Op. Cit., 26-41.

23. Ruth Rabbah 6:1.

24. Targum Ruth 3:8.

25. Ruth Rabbah 7:10.

26. Berlin, Adele "Ruth and the Continuity of Israel" in *Reading Ruth.*, Op. Cit., 255-260.

27. Pardes, Op. Cit., 98.

28. Klagsburn, F. Op. Cit., 272.

29. Berlin, Adele. Op. Cit., 258.

30. Ruth Rabbah 8:2.

CHAPTER FIVE:

EPILOGUE

I. CROSSING THE RIVER

II. OF KINGS AND GIANTS

III. A STORY FOR THE MORALS

He has let loose two oceans:
They meet one another.
Yet between them stands a barrier
which they cannot overrun.

–The Qur'an

CROSSING THE RIVER

The book of Ruth is simultaneously a classic journey story, a tale of female liberation, and a treatise on cultural blending. At the story's core is an exploration of what it means to leave home and go to another place. Both migrations in the book entail a crossing of the Jordan River which, in biblical times, marked a distinct passage.

The Jordan River (*the descender*) begins at Mt. Hermon and flows down to the Dead Sea. The mountains on either side are steep and sudden in contrast to the deep gorge cut by the river. The 200-mile river bends and loops through a 70-mile valley. Like the twists of the river, centuries of stories wind through history and explain the dynamic of life in the valley. Stories of community resettlement, personal transformation, supernatural encounters, and liberation surround the river and characterize life on its shores.

In the folk tradition surrounding the Jordan, there is a sense of awe for the opposite bank of the river. This sense may come from the fact that crossing the river implied a cleansing of the past or because different crops were grown on either side. Since the East Bank has more tributaries, it was famous for its fertile pastures. A dominant motif in river stories is a crossing catalyzed by famine or turbulence on the West Bank. While migration was common, the movement from one bank to the next was characterized by a meeting with the unknown.

In Islamic and Judaic milito-political texts, the river represents a clear demarcation of territory to be crossed in order to conquer "the enemy." Yet in the folk tradition of these two peoples, the river draws strangers together and allows for cultural exchange. The fertile soil made the valley a major crossroads of the Middle East where goods and customs were traded openly. Perhaps it is because the Jordan River Valley is a region of such prevalent cultural mixing that crossing the river came to represent a distinct passage.

River crossing stories address the fear of the other side. The unknown is manifest as a supernatural being or occurrence encountered by the protagonist; the supernatural symbolizes the unknown terrain and culture. By speaking of the demons or ghouls which inhabit a place, the fear of difference can be expressed. While the telling of such stories serves as an outlet, there is the danger of the story's perpetuation of stereotypes. In any case, crossing the river was believed to precede profound transformation, a perception which found its way into later Christian fable in which the crossing the Jordan was the path on which the devout entered heaven.

The book of Ruth begins as a Diaspora tale: a story of Israelites outside of their promised land. The Hebrew Bible is comprised to a large degree of Diaspora tales in which the protagonists wander around while all the time longing for the land of God's promise. The book of Ruth begins with one man's flight from Judah to Moab and his negative experience on the East Bank accentuates the tension between the two neighboring cultures. Ruth's absorption into Bethlehem resolves the tension on a microcosmic level. Because of her valor and her friendship with Naomi, Ruth is able to adjust and gain acceptance in a foreign land. The river is the gateway to her new life.

The relationship of Ruth and Naomi serves as a model for the bi-directional nature of cultural influence. Naomi lived in Moab for over ten years, adapted to the customs, and gained Ruth's alliance. She taught Ruth of her God, as evidenced by the repeated references to the Israelite deity. Amidst the collision of beliefs, the two women developed a friendship more powerful than difference. From Ruth, Naomi learned tenacity and independence. From Naomi, Ruth gained lessons of strategy and patience. The influence they exert on one another is so strong that they become like one person pursuing the same goal.

The Ghouleh of the Trans-Jordan, a Palestinian folk tale, is structurally identical to the book of Ruth. A poor man says to his family, "Let's cross over to Trans-Jordan; maybe we can find a better life there than we have here." The man takes his family, crosses the river, and discovers some deserted ruins. As he moves into an empty house, a woman approaches.

"Welcome!" she says to the man. "Welcome to my nephew! Since my brother died, you haven't dropped in on me, nor have you visited me."

In strange territory, the man is greeted as a relative and scolded for not having paid an earlier visit. The man assures his new-found aunt that he has arrived at the deserted village purely by chance. She responds by ushering him into a house well-stocked with food, thus curing his poverty. As in the case of Elimelech and the fields of Moab, an absence (famine, poverty) is filled by migration. Initially, resettlement proves beneficial. The man establishes a new life with his wife and daughter who are not mentioned in the act of traveling.

The wife and daughter cook meals and each evening, and the daughter takes a meal across the village to her aunt. Paralleling the book of Ruth, the second generation makes more direct contact with the host culture. Mahlon and Chilion marry Moabite women. The daughter in the Palestinian story explores the town and visits with her aunt each day. She exhibits her ability to adapt and to watch out for herself.

One evening, the daughter arrives at the woman's door and finds her transformed into a ghouleh. The woman/ghouleh has thrown "a young man with braid like those of a girl gone astray" to the ground and is devouring him. Betraying no shock, the girl steps back and calls out, "Hey, Aunty!" giving the ghouleh enough time to shake herself and assume the form of a woman.

The ghouleh reads fear on the girl's face and offers a phrase of protection, "the name of Allah protect you, niece!" The girl, without lying, explains that a black shape crossed her path and frightened her. Although the woman promises to stay at home, she follows the girl to hear her report.

"How's your aunt?" the mother asks on the girl's return.

Knowing that ghoulehs always follow their suspects, the girl tells a false story. Only when she is sure that the ghouleh is out of earshot does she reveal her aunt's identity. The daughter unveils the dark element of the town to her mother. The mother follows suit by relaying the discovery to her husband. She wakes him from a slumber, saying, "Get up, get up! It turns out your aunt is a ghouleh."

"What! My aunt a ghouleh! You're a ghouleh!" he responds.

The wife leaves her husband to his sleep and obstinacy, telling him that her claim was made in jest. She then calls her daughter, gathers food, and embarks on her own road to return.

After mother and daughter begin the journey home, the story returns to the sleeping man. Upon waking, he discovers the absence of his wife and daughter and acknowledges the present danger. Rather than escape, he hides himself in a flour bin. After sunrise, the ghouleh appears at his house and sees no one. She begins to dance and sing an odd lamentation: "My oil and my flour, O what a loss! Gone are the masters of the house!" The man in the flour bin becomes so terrified that he farts, scattering flour everywhere. The ghouleh opens the bin and asks where she should begin eating him. As he faces his end, the man realizes his mistakes. "Eat my little hand that did not listen to my little daughter." After eating his hand, the ghouleh asks which limb she should next eat. "Eat my beard," he answers, "that did not listen to my wife." In this manner, she eats him all.

The story catches up to the girl and her mother who have reached their home. The mother suspects that the ghouleh will pursue them and wreck further havoc on the family. Like Naomi, she feels cursed by her husband's migration. The mother predicts that the ghouleh will appear at the house disguised as a dog. When the dog appears, she instructs her daughter to pour a pot of olive oil on its head. The woman/dog/ghouleh arrives and is scalded to death with oil.

The following morning, the mother goes public with her knowledge. She tells all her neighbors about the abandoned town full of provisions that was once protected by a ghouleh. Offering the provisions to anyone strong enough to make the journey, she resolves to be satisfied with home.

In Arabic folklore, the *ghul* or ghouleh is considered to be a creature inferior to the Jinn, demons made of fire. It is commonly regarded as a form of Shaitan (Satan) who eats men and can assume various forms. The *ghul* haunt burial grounds and devour any ill-fortuned person who crosses their path. In Bedouin lore, the *ghul* usually appears as an animal who makes terrible noises at dusk. Al-Jahiz speaks of marrying a woman *ghul* who ran away from him into the desert.[1] In pre-Islamic time, a *ghul* was a female demon who assumed the form of a beautiful woman. Later, a *ghul* was believed to be a demon who lived a solitary, desert existence and disguised itself as a person traveling. The companions of the prophet are said to have encountered *ghul* on their travels.

In the Lisan al-A'rab, *ghilun*, means a death or destruction caused by alcohol and in the Quran, it is defined as a headache one has after drinking heavily. In Hadith, the prophet makes a statement that three things can rule over one's life: anger, greed, and pride (much of it). These are manifestations of the inner devil, *ghul,*, which can penetrate the soul.[2]

In our story, the ghouleh reigns over a place of seeming abundance. She makes the man and his family feel comfortable and only attacks after her true identity has been discovered. The man is devoured by the ghouleh in the same manner that Elimelech and his sons are subsumed in the darkness of Moab's fields. The ghouleh personifies the danger inherent in any resettlement and the piece by piece manner in which she devours the man corresponds with the nature of assimilation. Neither the book of Ruth nor *The Ghouleh of the Trans-Jordan* are anti-travel stories. Rather, they address the loss involved with any change, especially the departure from home and community.

In both stories, family composition is altered by eastward movement. The men meet with death which places women in positions of autonomy. The similarity between the two stories is further evidence of the book of Ruth's oral beginnings. The similarities between the two stories suggest that the tale of two women returning from the east bank was a popular one among the different peoples living in the river valley. The more detailed biblical story provides a more extensive portrait of cultural blending. If the story ended with Elimelech and his sons dying in the fields of Moab, then the moral would be the same as the folktale's: be satisfied with what you have. But the majority of the biblical story is concerned with how Ruth the Moabite successfully resettles on the other side of the river. On one level, the contrast between Elimelech's death in Moab and Ruth's fulfillment in Bethlehem implies a belief in cultural superiority. Yet, the primary lesson in the book of Ruth is the importance of accepting strangers. Ruth maintains her identity as "the Moabite" throughout her stay in Bethlehem. Because of her difference, Ruth introduces new virtues into the town and through her personal strength, she overcomes cultural barriers.

The daughter in *The Ghouleh of the Trans-Jordan* is a hero comparable to Ruth. Exhibiting cleverness and calm, she traverses the deserted village, sees beyond her "aunt's" hospitality, and saves her and her mother's lives. In her return home and outsmarting of the ghouleh, her journey becomes cyclic and redemptive. Although she loses her father, the lessons learned on the other side of the Jordan impact the rest of her life. To confront a ghouleh and survive is an act of transcendence, a return from darkness.

OF KINGS AND GIANTS:
SPLIT AND RECONCILIATION BETWEEN ISRAEL AND MOAB

Like David and Goliath, modernity and ancient Judaism face each other in wonder, both believing themselves to be giants.

On the other side of the river, Naomi and her family face a specific unknown. They meet with Moabites, people with whom the children of Israel had an ongoing saga of fear and attraction. The Moabites were long-time neighbors, believed to be distant relatives descended from Lot. They worshipped many gods, primarily Chemosh, the god of sun and war, and Ashtar, the mother goddess, in ecstatic ritual. Often tempted by incense and abandon the Israelites would participate in Moabite rituals, only to be punished by their own, more wrathful God. Like a jealous lover, God would not endure other attractions. Going to Moab carried connotations of entering a land of forbidden pleasures. The entrance was made again and again.

Abraham and Lot depart from their home and wander together as strangers in a strange land. Early on, the two kinsmen part ways because "the land could not support them both together" (Gen. 13:6). Furthermore, their livestock was too numerous to allow for collective settlement and "there were quarrels between Abram's herdsmen and Lot's," euphemisms for the fact that the two men had distinctly different agendas (Gen. 13:7).

When they can no longer travel together, Abraham offers Lot whatever region he desires. Lot chooses the fertile Jordan River Valley. Hoping for an easy life, he takes an eastward route and settles in Sodom. Abraham remains on the outskirts of society, conducting his dialogue with God in the wilderness. As Lot walks into the distance, God appears to Abraham and promises him: "All the land you can see I will give to you and your descendants for ever. Now go through the length and breadth of the land, for I give it to you" (Gen. 13:15-17). Abraham is instructed by God to wander through the land and dream of a future when his descendants will populate it. In the meantime, he is severed from his extended family and must begin a new tribe in an alien land. Abraham still cares for Lot and rushes to his nephew's rescue when he is carried off as a prisoner of war.

Lot and Abraham are visited by the same angels. Abraham is promised a child in one year's time. Lot is warned of the destruction about to fall on his city. When the angels appear at Sodom's gate, Lot exhibits a hospitality contrary to his environment. He invites them to spend the night at his house and insists when they refuse. Before his guests lie down to sleep, the men of Sodom surround Lot's house and demanded that the visitors be brought out, in order for the men to "have intercourse with them" (Gen. 19:5).

Lot, without hesitation, offers his two virgin daughters as substitutes: "Look, I have two daughters, both virgins; let me bring them out to you, and you can do what you like with them; but do not touch these men, because they have come under the shelter of my roof" (Gen. 19:6-9). Lot guards his guests and pawns his daughters, placing the assumed role of host above fatherhood. The crowd refuses the substitution and presses in. The angels pull Lot inside and strike the crowd with blindness. They urge Lot to leave the city immediately, but he hesitates until the angels grab his hand and lead him away.

After Sodom has been destroyed by fire and Lot's wife has been transformed into a pillar of salt, Lot and his daughters settle in a mountain cave. The daughters turn Lot's plan back on him by using their father for his sperm. Believing that all other men on earth have burned, they sleep with their father to ensure their own continuity. The older daughter formulates the plan: "Our father is old and there is not a man in the country to come to us in the usual way. Come now, let us make our father drink wine and then lie with him, and in this way keep the family alive through our father" (Gen. 19:31-33). The daughters get their father drunk and sleep with him on subsequent nights. The younger daughter gives birth to a son, Ben-ammi, ancestor of the Ammonites and the older daughter gives birth to Moab, ancestor of the Moabites. "Moab" means "from the father."

The story of Lot and his daughters deals unabashedly with incest. The daughters cross the boundaries of propriety in order to keep the family name alive. They are empowered as they turn the tables on a father who treated them like expendable prostitutes. This account of Moab's origin may well be an Israelite construct which serves to demonize the Moabites. Being the descendants of Lot implies a legacy of shortsightedness and their incestuous origin places the Moabites in the category of being "unclean." The story may have been created to perpetuate the Hebrew belief in cultural superiority.

When the people of Israel encounter the Moabites during their wanderings, they are instructed by God: "Do not harass the Moabites nor provoke them to battle, or I will not give you any of their land as a possession" (Deut. 2:9). Moabite land is not to be touched or coveted. Designated for Lot's descendants, it is protected by an alternate promise. While the Moabites are not to be provoked, they are not to be accepted.

No Ammonite or Moabite, even down to the tenth generation, shall become a member of the assembly of the Lord. They shall never become members of the assembly of the Lord, because they hired Balaam son of Beor from Pethor in Aram-naharaim to revile you. The Lord your God refused to listen to Balaam and turned his denunciation into a blessing, because the Lord your God loved you. You shall never seek their welfare or their good all your life long (Deut. 23:3-6).

The prohibition against accepting Moabites stems from an incident that appears in Numbers 22. The Israelites camp in the fields of Moab, causing a wave of fear to run through the Moabite population. Balak, king of Moab, summons Balaam, Mesopotamia's most reputable sorcerer, to curse the newly arrived tribes. Balaam twice refuses the King's summons, but accompanies his messengers on the third request. God tells Balaam to go with the messengers, but becomes angry when he departs. Balaam and his donkey encounter an angel on the road who tells the sorcerer to speak only the words dictated to him by God. King Balak hastily greets Balaam and takes him up three different mountains in order for him to view the people of Israel and curse them. From each vantage point, Balaam can only utter words of blessing.

After this incident, the people of Israel camp in the plains of Moab where they realize their attraction to Moabite women.

> The people began to have intercourse with Moabite women who invited them to the sacrifices offered to their gods; and they ate the sacrificial food and prostrated themselves before the gods of Moab. The Israelites joined in the worship of the Baal of Peor, and the Lord was angry with them (Num. 25:1-4).

Every participant in the ritual is put to death as part of a lesson not to worship other gods. The relationship between the liberated Israelites and the Moabites is as difficult as that of Abraham and Lot. The large scale massacre in the fields of Moab informs the later deaths of Elimelech and his sons.

The relationship between Ruth and Naomi and the relationship between Ruth and Boaz represent a tremendous narrative reconciliation. Ruth the Moabite is a heroine who marries one of Bethlehem's most prominent men. She begins the Davidic line. The great King David openly acknowledges the Moabite blood in his veins. When Saul relentlessly pursues David, David goes to Moab and asks the Moabite King to provide sanctuary for his mother and father. David's parents remain at the court of Moab until the danger passes. The alliance is later ignored when David attacks and humiliates the Moabites.

> He defeated the Moabites, and he made them lie along the ground and measured them off with a length of cord; for every two lengths that were to be put to death one full length was spared. The Moabites became subject to him and paid him tribute (II Samuel 8:2-3).

With the attack, David denies his genetic connection to the Moabites and subjects them to a cruel form of subjugation and death. By wiping out a percentage of the Moabites, he may well be trying to deny his own Moabite ancestry. Solomon mends the rift caused by his father when he marries a Moabite princess and builds "a hill shrine for Kemosh ... on the height to the east of Jerusalem" (I Kings, 11:7). By incorporating Moabite worship into his vision of an inclusive kingdom, he acknowledges the validity of Moabite practice.

A split precedes Ruth's surrender to Naomi's life. Ruth and Orpah (who in rabbinic literature are both the daughters of Eglon, King of Moab) part ways. Orpah disappears and is not reported on further, while Ruth migrates to Bethlehem. Whether or not they are sisters in the literal sense, the two women have been married to brothers, have adapted to Israelites customs, and have lived side by side for at least ten years. Initially, they use one voice to cry out to Naomi. When Ruth and Orpah diverge, it is as decisive a split as that between Abraham and Lot. The two women go different ways and give rise to two different peoples.

According to Rabbinic literature, when David and Goliath stand facing each other, it is another confrontation between Israel and

Moab.[3] Orpah is identified with Harafa, the mother of Goliath and three other Philistine giants (2 Samuel 21:19-22). The four sons were given to Orpah for the four times she shed tears when parting with Naomi. Ruth and Orpah meet again in the forms of a shepherd and a giant. As women, they walk their ways. As men, they do battle.

Abraham and Lot engage in another dance of distances in the form of Ruth and Orpah. According to legend, Ruth and Orpah reconfront each other as David and Goliath. The cycle of split and reconciliation between Israel and Moab explores what it means to be neighbors. A classic neighbor scenario, the Israelites held a grudge, harbored a secret attraction, and thought that they were superior to the Moabites. In any case, there was no escaping the relationship. The repeated meetings of Israel and Moab teach that enemies and fears do not disappear, but need to be confronted time and time again. Since Moabite land was initially not to be conquered, the Israelites had to negotiate their desire and distrust. David disgraced the Moabites; Solomon imitated them. In light of Israel's and Moab's tenuous relationship, Ruth's and Naomi's commitment to one another points to a plausible cultural reconciliation.

A STORY FOR THE MORALS

The commandments brought down from the mountain by Moses provide guidelines, a ten-step program of what should and shouldn't be done. The people of Israel need guidance in order to shed their slave mentality and claim their freedom. Since escaping Egypt, all they've done is complain about the lack of water and food. "If only we had died at the Lord's hand in Egypt, where we sat round the fleshpots and had plenty of bread to eat! But you have brought us out into this wilderness to let this whole assembly starve to death" (Ex. 16:3). The people accuse Moses of leading them into the wilderness to share in a group death. They turn their anxieties on their leader and glorify their past. Moses relays the complaint of hunger to God who answers it with the presentation of Manna. Manna which tastes "like a wafer made with honey" falls with the dew each morning. It fills the people's hunger and attests to God's presence: "In the morning you will see the glory of the Lord, because He has heeded your complaints against him; it is not against us that you bring your complaints; we are nothing" (Ex. 16:7-8). Trying to expand the people's ken, Moses refers to himself as the intermediary between them and a larger power and begins instruction on how to look beyond the physical. Having encountered God directly, Moses' beliefs are based on experience. The people have not had a parallel experience; they are slaves used to measuring pleasure and displeasure in terms of physical pain. In order to believe in their security or blessedness, they require tangible proof. Despite Moses' claim that he is only a medium, the people direct their doubts toward him.

When Jethro, Moses' father-in-law meets him in the wilderness, he criticizes Moses' leadership. Why, Jethro inquires, must the people come to Moses for God's guidance. He suggests a democratic solution:

> It is for you to be the people's representative before God, and bring their disputes to Him. You must instruct them in the statutes and laws, and teach them how they must behave and what they must do. But you must yourself search for capable, God-fearing men among all the people, honest and incorruptible men, and appoint them over the people as officers ... If you do this, God will give you strength, and you will be able to go on. And, moreover, this whole people will here and now regain peace and harmony (Ex. 18:19-23).

Jethro proposes the delegation of power as a means of involving the people in their own fate. Moses heeds his advice, appoints officers, and establishes a social order.

The people wander on. When they arrive at Mount Sinai, Moses ascends into the smoke and fire on the mountain top, leaving the people alone. He pursues his individual vision without invitation or explanation. The people fear the thunder and lightening and feel abandoned as their leader disappears into a dark cloud. Moses comes down from the mountain carrying rules intended to bind the people together with common belief. Through the transmission of principle, he hopes to fill the void of their faith. The commandments are intended as moral parameters dictated by God.

As Moses approaches the camp with his tablets of rules, he hears singing. Rather than welcome the sound of a collective voice raised in celebration, he becomes enraged. Moses sees the golden calf surrounded by ecstatic dancing as a sign of the people's moral ineptitude. Moses shuts down the party, grinds the golden calf into powder, and forces the Israelites to drink it.

Aaron tries to quell his brother's anger by explaining that the calf represents no great transgression, only the people's need for divine manifestation. "Aaron replied, 'Do not be angry, sir. The people were deeply troubled; that you well know. And they said to me, "Make us gods to go ahead of us, because, as for this fellow Moses, who brought us up from Egypt, we do not know what has become of him"'" (Ex. 32:22-24). According to Aaron, the people's desire for a God to "go ahead" of them is a direct response to Moses' absence. The people, not invited to meet with the God veiled by thunder and smoke, created a god they could see and dance for. Other than complaining, worship of the golden calf is the first thing that the people do together. Participation in the group ritual is an expression of freedom and solidarity.

Venting his fury, Moses flings down the tablets and literally breaks the commandments. He then orders the Levites to: "Arm yourselves, each of you, with his sword. Go through the camp from gate to gate and back again. Each of you kill his brother, his friend, his neighbour" (Ex. 32:27). As three thousand people die in the massacre, the sixth commandment is broken. Creation of the golden calf reveals an essential crisis between the vision of Moses and the vision of the people. Moses wants the people to believe in the concept of justice and the alliance of an invisible God. To him, freedom extends beyond a few hours of abandon and entails responsibility. He offers the commandments to ritualize everyday life and teach moral self-sufficiency. The people, disenfranchised from any societal structure, hunger for the stability of a physical god. They want a golden deity and the revelry of release.

Before the journey through the wilderness progresses, the visions of Moses and the people are blended. God commands the creation of the tent of the Presence and the Tabernacle. When Moses enters the tent, God's pillar of cloud descends for as long as the prophet and the deity engage in dialogue. The people, upon seeing the cloud drop, would "prostrate themselves, every man at the entrance to his tent" (Ex. 33:11). The need for group worship is fulfilled as the people participate in the creation of a mobile religion:

> Let all who wish, bring a contribution to the Lord: gold, silver, copper; violet, purple, and scarlet yarn; fine linen and goats' hair; tanned rams' skins, porpoise-hides, and acacia wood; ... Let every craftsman among you come and make everything the Lord has commanded (Ex. 35:5-10).

By providing the people with visual indications of God, Moses quiets their anxiety. The tabernacle combines the people's need for tangible divinity with Moses' concept of God. The stone rules are carried in a golden case.

Moses' ten principles have been passed down as the basis of western morality. The Jewish holiday of Shavuot (Pentecost) commemorates the wheat harvest as well as Moses' delivery of the commandments. The commandments, like the harvest, give proof of God's presence;

it is through a combination of wheat and principle that people thrive. While the wheat harvest plays a prominent role in the book of Ruth, the reason for its recitation on Shavuot is often called into question.

For centuries, Jewish commentators have struggled to make the connection. "And what is for Ruth with Pentecost that it is read in the revelation on Mt. Sinai? To teach you that the Torah is given only with tribulation."[4] In this explanation, Naomi's and Ruth's trials are an extension of their having received the Torah. While the Torah was not brought down to them from a mountain, Naomi received it in terms of a legacy which she passed to Ruth. "Receiving the Torah" means adhering to a code of conduct which is tested and altered under the duress of daily life. Ruth and Naomi exhibit strength and courage in their response to tribulation. As they overcome hardship, they receive God's blessing.

Another commentary states:

Now it came to pass in the days (vayye-hee) when Judges judged that there was (vayye-hee) a famine in the land ... Why is it written twice vayye-hee? One for the bread and one for the Torah to teach you that a generation without the Torah is destined to have famine.[5]

This interpretation reasons that tribulation results from an absence of Torah. Separation from God's code creates a state of famine, as in the case of Elimelech. According to this model, Torah acts as a shield, while its loss invites disaster. Thus the famine in the book of Ruth is caused by the lack of "Torah," or the lack of moral behavior. The deaths of Elimelech and his sons can be explained in a similar manner: their flight from civic responsibility caused their deaths.

The ten commandments are a list of laws, practical guidelines of how to behave. While their phrasing is straightforward, implementation of the commandments raises questioning and ambiguities. The book of Ruth which shows how people embody virtue is a story for the morals. It fills in the commandments through narrative example. The commandments come to life as characters who face the real challenges of hunger and homelessness, loneliness and age. Elimelech, his sons, and Orpah serve as examples of how not to act and stand in direct contrast to the characters of Ruth, Naomi, and Boaz. Operating together, the ten commandments and the book of Ruth illustrate belief and action.

Midrashic writers attest to the book of Ruth's impact. "For what purpose then was it written? To teach us how great is the reward of those who do deeds of kindness."[6] According to the Midrash, the book of Ruth boils down to kindness. Ruth's virtue is rewarded in her lifetime and is passed as a legacy to King David. Ruth, a feminine parallel to Moses, gives the people a timeless example of moral action.

Ruth and Moses have much the same job. Moses must answer the people's doubt and "fill" them through the transmission of principle. Ruth "fills" Naomi's spiritual famine with Judean crops and the birth of an heir. In this capacity, Moses and Ruth are similar mediums, able to bring "Torah" to people who lack it. The cycle of return corresponds in the two stories. The people of Israel cross a body of water (Red Sea), wander a landscape of challenge (wilderness of Sinai), and are restored to nationhood by receiving the principles from the mountain. Naomi and Ruth cross the Jordan River, walk the road from Moab to Bethlehem, and are restored as a family by the birth of Obed. The transmission of law and barley, instruction and emotion is an act of connecting heaven and earth.

Revelation is a trip up a mountain. The individual meets with God and brings down principles. The law received at the mountain's top is meant to give order to ex-slaves who find themselves in the wilderness. The transmission of principle from Moses to the people of Israel "fills" them and provides guidance in the expanse of the desert. It brings them back to life, or back to a life as an autonomous people. By having guidelines, they have parameters in which to function. God's presence is communicated in the presentation of the commandments. Revelation is an expedition to the fields. One woman, a stranger goes out to the fields and gathers barley. She brings it to her mother-in-law who has been deprived of food grown in her native land. Naomi is given life by Ruth's offering.

The stories of the man on the mountain and the woman in the fields are based on the transformations of summer. Moses' ascent and Ruth's "going out" parallel the seasonal shift. The hotter and longer days of summer invite an exfoliation of self. The stories of Moses and Ruth are read on the spring harvest holiday to reveal the spiritual significance of the season, for summer is a time of elevation and transfiguration. Biblical stories, each assigned to a calendar day, point to the stages of the yearly cycle. The stories reflect nature, thereby teaching about human nature. The acknowledgment of seasonal shifts reveals similar change in the individual psyche. Revelation is in the acknowledgment that internal changes mirror external ones.

Appendix III:
The Ghouleh of Transjordan

Once there was a poor man. One day he said to his family. "Let's cross over to Trans-Jordan. Maybe we can find a better life there than we have here." They had (May Allah preserve your worth!) a beast of burden.

Crossing eastward, they came upon some deserted ruins. When they found an empty house in the ruins, they wanted to move into it. A woman came upon them. "Welcome!" she said to the man. "Welcome to my nephew! Since my brother died, you haven't dropped in on me, nor have you visited me."

"By Allah," he answered, "my father never mentioned you to me. And in any case, we came here only by chance."

"Welcome!" she replied. "Welcome! Go ahead and stay in this house." Now, the house was well stocked with food, and they settled in. The man had only his wife and a daughter. They would cook meals, and in the evening the daughter took the woman her dinner. She lived in the southern part of the ruined town, and they lived in the north, with some distance between them.

One evening the girl went to bring the woman her dinner. She came up to the door, and lo! the woman had thrown to the ground a young man with braids like those of a girl gone astray, and she was devouring him. Stepping back, the girl moved some distance away and called out, "Hey, Aunty! Aunty!" The ghouleh shook herself, taking the shape of a woman again, and came to the terrified girl.

"The name of Allah protect you, niece!" exclaimed the ghouleh.

"A black shape crossed my path," the girl explained, "and I became frightened."

Taking the dinner from the girl, the ghouleh said, "Don't worry!

I'll wait here until you get inside the house." But she followed her to the door of the house to find out what the girl was going to say to her mother.

"How's your aunt?" asked the mother.

Now the girl was a clever one, and she answered, "When I got there, I found her sitting quietly with her head in her lap, like this."

After the ghouleh had gone back to her house to finish what she was eating, the girl said to her mother, "Mother, it turns out our aunt is a ghouleh."

"How do you know she's a ghouleh?" asked the mother.

"I saw her eating a lad with locks like those of a seductive girl," said the girl.

Her husband was sleeping. "Get up, get up!" she said. "It turns out your aunt is a ghouleh."

"What! My aunt a ghouleh! You're a ghouleh!"

"All right," the wife replied. "Sleep, sleep!" We were only joking with you."

When he had gone back to sleep, they went and filled a sack with flour. They brought a tin can full of olive oil and (May it be far from the listeners!) the beast of burden. Loading the provisions on it, they called upon the Everlasting to watch over their journey.

Meanwhile, the man slept till morning, and when he woke he found neither wife nor daughter. "So," he thought, "it seems what they said is true." He mounted to the top of the flour bin and lowered himself in.

After sunrise, the ghouleh showed up, but when she went into the house, there was no one there. Turning herself back into a ghouleh, she started dancing and singing: "My oil and my flour, O what a loss! Gone are the masters of the house!"

When he heard her singing and prancing about, the man was so scared he farted, scattering flour dust into the air. She saw him.

"Ah!" she cried out. "You're still here!"

"Yes, Aunty!" he answered.

"Well come down here," she said. "Where shall I start eating you?"

"Eat my little hand," he answered, "that did not listen to my little daughter."

After eating his hand, she asked again, "Where shall I eat you now?"

And so on, until she devoured him all.

Now we go back to the girl and her mother. When they had reached home, the mother said to her daughter, "She's bound to follow us and turn herself (God save your honors!) into a bitch. She'll scratch against the door. I'll boil a pot full of olive oil, and you open for her. When she comes in, I'll pour the oil over her head."

In a while the ghouleh came and scratched at the door, and the girl opened for her. No sooner had she gone in the door than the woman poured the oil onto her head. She exploded, and behold! she was dead. There was no moisture in her eye.

In the morning the woman filled the town with her shouts, and people rushed to her rescue.

"What's the matter?" they asked.

"Listen," she said. "There's a ruin, and it's full of provisions. It was protected by a ghouleh, and here! I've killed the ghouleh. Any one who has strength can go load up on wheat, flour, and oil. As for me, I'll be satisfied with the food in the house where we stayed."

Notes

Chapter five: Epilogue

1. *The Holy Qu'ran* 37:47.
2. *Lisan al-A'rab.*

3. Yalkut, 600.
4. Yalkut, 596.
5. Yalkut, 597.
6. Ruth Rab. 2:14.

References

Alter, Robert. 1981. *The Art of Biblical Narrative*. New York: Basic Books.

Anderson, A.A. 1978. "The Marriage of Ruth," *Journal of Semitic Studies, Vol. 23*

Anderson, Sherry Ruth and Patricia Hopkins. 1991. *The Feminine Face of God*. Bantan Books.

Atkinson, David. 1983. *The Wings of Refuge: The Message of Ruth*. Intervarsity Press.

Barton, G.A. 1905. "Ruth Rabbah." *Jewish Encyclopedia, Vol. 10*.

Battan, Israel. 1950. "The Five Scrolls, A Commentary" *Union of American Hebrew Congregations*.

Beattie, D.R.G. 1985. "The Targum of Ruth–A Sectarian Composition?" *The Journal of Jewish Studies, Vol. 26*.

The Bible, Jerusalem. 1992. Jerusalem: Koren Publishers.

The Bible, New English. 1970. Oxford University Press.

Boyarin, Daniel. 1993. *Carnal Israel*. Berkeley: University of California Press.

Brenner, Athalya, ed. 1993. *A Feminist Companion to Ruth*. Sheffield Academic Press.

Brown, Norman O. 1966. *Love's Body*. Berkeley: University of California Press.

Buechner, Frederick. 1993. *Son of Laughter*. San Francisco: Harper.

Burrows, Millar. 1940. "The Marriage of Boaz and Ruth," *Journal of Biblical Literature 50*.

Campbell, Joseph. 1973. *The Hero with a Thousand Faces*. New Jersey: Princeton University Press.

Cooke, G.A. 1918. *The Book of Ruth*. Cambridge: University Press.

Craghan, John. 1982. *Esther, Judith, Tobit, Jonah, Ruth*. Wilmington, DE.

Dante. *Inferno*. Sinclair, John D., trans. 1939. New York: Oxford University Press.

Dickstein, Morris. 1977. *Gates of Eden*. New York: Penguin.

Frye, Northrop. 1966. *Fables of Identity: Studies in Poetic Mythology*. Harvest Books.

Gage, Warren Austin. 1989. "Ruth upon the Threshing Floor and the Sin of Gibeah: A Biblical-Theological Study." *The Westminster Theological Journal, Vol. 51*.

Ginzberg, Louis. 1956. *Legends of the Bible*. Philadelphia: Jewish Publication Society.

Goitein, S.D. 1957. "Megilat Ruth" In *Omanut ha-Sippur ba-Mikra 2*. Jerusalem.

Gordon, A.R. 1912. *The Poets of the Old Testament*. Hodder and Stoughton.

Graetz, Naomi. 1993. *S/He Created Them: Feminist Retellings of Biblical Stories*. New Jersey: Menorah House.

Graves, Robert. 1955. *The Greek Myths*. Baltimore: Penguin Books.

Hirshfield, Jane. 1994. *Women in Praise of the Sacred*. New York: HarperPerennial.

Hubbard, Robert. 1988. *The Book of Ruth*. Grand Rapids: Eerdman's Publishing.

Kates, Judith and Gail Twersky Reimer, eds. 1994. *Reading Ruth*. New York: Ballantine Books.

Kerouac, Jack. 1955. *On the Road*. New York: Signet.

The Koran., trans. Dawood, N.J. 1956. Penguin Books.

Josephus. 1985. *Complete Works*. Kregel Publications.

Lee, Peter K.H. "Two Stories of Loyalty." *Ching Feng*, Vol. 32.

Levine, Etan. 1973. *The Aramaic Version of Ruth*. Rome: Biblical Institute Press.

MacKinnon, Catharine. 1987. *Feminism Unmodified*. Cambridge: Harvard University Press.

Mandelbaum, Allen, trans. 1961. *The Aeneid of Virgil*. Bantam Books.

May, H.G. 1984. *Oxford Bible Atlas*. New York: Oxford University Press.

Mitchell, Stephen. 1987. Introduction. *The Book of Job*. San Francisco: North Point Press.

Muhani, Ibrahim and Sharif Kanaana. 1989. *Speak Bird, Speak Again: Palestinian Arab Folktales*. Berkeley: University of California Press.

Pardes, Ilana. 1992. *Countertraditions in the Bible: A Feminist Approach*. Cambridge: Harvard University Press.

Patai, Raphael. 1967. *The Hebrew Goddess*. Detroit: Wayne State University Press.

Phipps, W.E. 1992. *Assertive Biblical Women*. Westport: Greenwood Press.

Pritchard, James. 1974. *Solomon and Sheba*. Londond: Phaidon.

Sasson, Jack. 1979. *Ruth: A New Translation with a Philological Commentary and a Formalist-Folklorist Interpretation*. Baltimore: Johns Hopkins University Press.

Spilenger, Paul. 1992. "Dante's Arte and the Ambivalence of Retrospection." In *Stanford Italian Review vol. x:2*.

Stanton, Elizabeth Cady. 1981. *The Woman's Bible*. Seattle: Coalition Task Force on Women and Religion.

Teubal, Savina. 1984. *Sarah the Priestess: The First Matriarch of Genesis*. Athens: Swallow Press.

_____. 1990. *Hagar the Egyptian*. New York: Harper and Row.

_____. 1994. "The Genesis Narratives: Told by Women, Written by Men?" an unpublished article presented at SBL meeting, Chicago.

Trible, Phyllis. 1976. "Two Women in a Man's World: A Reading of the Book of Ruth." *Soundings* 59.

Vallas, B.M. 1954. "The Book of Ruth and Its Purpose." *Theologia* 25.

Zenger, Erich. 1991. *Das Buch Ruth*. Zurich: Heirich Schmid and Siegfried Schultz.